Creative
Woodturning

Creative Woodturning

Dale L. Nish

Brigham Young University Press

Library of Congress Cataloging in Publication Data

Nish, Dale, 1932—
        Creative woodturning; a how-to book for lathe
craftsmen.

        1. Turning.   I. Title.
TT201.N56   684'.083   75-6952
ISBN 0-8425-0469-9
ISBN 0-8425-1557-7 pbk.
ISBN 0-8425-0472-9 (special)

Library of Congress Catalog Card Number: 75-6952
International Standard Book Number: 0-8425-0469-9 (cloth)
                                    0-8425-1557-7 (paper)
                                    0-8425-0472-9 (special)
Brigham Young University Press, Provo, Utah 84602
© 1975 Brigham Young University Press. All rights reserved.
Second printing 1976
Printed in the United States of America
76   8M   19298

Contents

Foreword

To those who use a woodturning lathe, whether they are amateur or professional, and to those who teach the use of a woodturning lathe, *Creative Woodturning* will be an invaluable resource.

The author addresses himself to the task of illustrating and elaborating on the machinery, tools, materials, processes, and techniques of woodturning. The book includes more than 580 photographs dealing with step-by-step procedures accompanying the written text to clarify each operation. In addition to this, more than 100 photographs in the project section show innovative project ideas covering both ends of the spectrum—from a very basic turning to a highly complex turning.

This book has to be the most comprehensive book on contemporary wood lathe turning available. The book contains many of the little known aids used to save time and achieve professional results.

Robert G. Trout
California State University
Long Beach, California

The Wood Lathe

Wood turning is one of the oldest applications of power to a machine. It is an operation where machine power is combined with the skill of hand tool work, and the art and design possessed by the operator. The combination of hand tool work and power make the lathe a versatile and interesting machine. It is one of the few woodworking machines capable of producing finished articles. The combining of lathe work and craftsmanship lead to the production of beautiful pieces of work.

The art of wood turning requires skill and practice on the part of the operator, as the quality of the product depends on the ability of the worker to use the tools. A knowledge of basic design principles is also required to produce articles of beauty and integrity. This knowledge of design, combined with a knowledge of the characteristics of wood, and practice in the turning operations, will enable the worker to become a skilled wood turner.

With practice the worker will soon be confident at the lathe, and will be able to produce articles of beauty and lasting value.

Wood turning as a trade is limited to a few people in the woodworking industry. This is because modern turning machines can automatically produce up to several thousand pieces per hour, with accuracy difficult to achieve by hand. However, the art of wood turning is still necessary for the model maker, pattern maker, furniture restorer, or home craftsman.

Fig. 2. The size of the lathe is determined by two factors:

1. The swing of the lathe is twice the distance from the center of the spindle to the bed of the lathe. The swing is the largest diameter which can be turned on the lathe.

2. The distance between centers is the maximum length of stock which can be turned on the lathe.

Fig. 3. Many types of lathes are available; however, the most common is the standard wood turning lathe, of which there are many models.

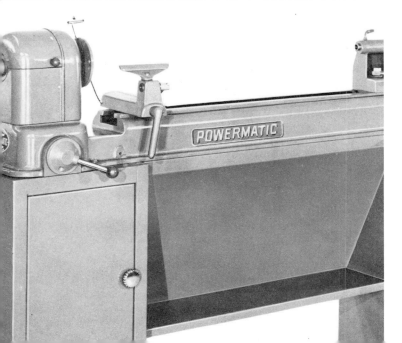

Some standard wood lathes are available with a gap-bed. This feature is useful for faceplate turning, as the maximum turning diameter may be increased from 12 inches over the straight bed to 17 inches over the gap.

Fig. 4. Some lathes are belt driven, with step pulleys allowing the operator to change speeds.

Common speeds for four step pulleys are approximately 900, 1300, 2100, and 3200 rpm.

Other lathes such as the Powermatic models 45 and 90 have variable speed pulleys, which change diameter according to the speed dialed by the operator. These pulleys are enclosed in a guard, and are not visible to the operator unless the guard has been removed.

LATHE SPEEDS

Lathe speeds are controlled in various ways. However, it is good judgment to select a lathe which can be started only at the lowest speed, preferably around 350 rpm. The best speed for turning is not easily determined, as several factors are involved:

1. Length and diameter of stock for spindle turning
2. Diameter and thickness of faceplate stock
3. Method of fastening stock to faceplate
4. Laminated or built-up stock

It is well to keep in mind that the actual speed of the work piece is determined by its diameter, as well as by the lathe speed. With two pieces of stock of different diameters, and the lathe set at the same speed, the work surface of the larger piece will come past the lathe tool several times faster than the work surface of the smaller piece.

IT IS NOT NECESSARY TO TURN AT HIGH SPEEDS. *Successful turning is the result of correct tool use, not high lathe speeds.*

Although it is common to increase the speed of the lathe for sanding and finishing, this is a poor practice which can cause accidents, particularly with laminated turnings. Sanding can be effectively completed at the same speed the stock was turned. A major problem with sanding is heat and friction, a problem which is increased by high speeds.

Spindle Turning

Long stock or small diameter spindle stock must be turned at low speeds, owing to problems with vibration and whipping. At high speeds, the stock may vibrate and form a shallow arc, much like a skipping rope. This causes the piece to shorten in length, with the possibility of being thrown from between the centers, with injury to the operator.

Large diameter stock must be turned at the lowest speeds, particularly during the roughing cuts, until the stock is balanced and cylindrical in shape. Large stock is often out of balance, and the heavy weight may cause excessive vibration, with a chance the stock will be thrown from the lathe. When stock is true and in balance, lathe speeds may be increased slightly.

Faceplate Turning

The diameter and thickness of the stock is important in determining turning speeds. Large or thick pieces must be rough turned at the lowest speeds to avoid excessive vibration because the stock is heavy and out of balance. When the stock has been rough turned, speed may be increased slightly, although the turning can often be completed at low speeds, particularly if it is over 5 or 6 inches in diameter.

The method of fastening stock to the faceplate is also important in determining safe speeds. Stock fastened to the faceplate with short screws, or by the glue method, must be turned at low speeds, as these fastening methods are not as secure as others. With proper care, however, no problems should be encountered.

Outboard turning with large diameter pieces is always at low speed. Even at low lathe speeds, the rim speed of the stock may be very high. Also, the outboard tool rest is not as secure as the tool rest fastened to the lathe bed, and the position of the tool rest must be watched continuously to prevent contact with the turning stock.

Laminated or Built-up Stock

This type of turning must be carefully glued, with no weak joints, or it may literally explode as a result of the centrifugal force of turning. Laminated pieces should always be turned at low speeds. Differences in grain direction, and the difference in hardness of several pieces of stock may also cause problems not associated with solid stock. It is well for the beginning turner to work with solid stock until the basic technique of turning has been mastered.

Fig. 5. **Headstock**—This assembly contains the driving mechanism for the lathe. It is bolted to the lathe bed and contains the spindle for the spur or live center.

The headstock may also contain the speed control, as well as the motor.

On some models, one pulley is also part of the headstock.

Fig. 6. **Tailstock**—The tailstock assembly is a unit which can be moved along the bed of the lathe and clamped at the desired distance from the headstock.

It contains the #2 morse taper spindle, tailstock handwheel, tailstock lock, and the dead or cup center, which is inserted into the tailstock spindle.

The cup center may be removed by turning the spindle all the way back. At this point, the cup center will contact a screw and be pushed out.

Fig. 7. **Lathe bed**—This is the part which supports the lathe. The headstock and tailstock assemblies are fastened to it, as well as the tool support base. The bed is also fastened to a stand, or base cabinet.

Tool support base and tool rest—The tool support base is clamped to the bed, and may be positioned where desired along the bed of the lathe. The tool support base contains a socket into which fits the tool rest. The tool rest may be moved up or down as required, or turned as needed for faceplate turning.

LATHE ACCESSORIES
Lathe Centers

Fig. 8. **Spur or drive center**—This center fits into the headstock spindle and drives the work when turning between centers. It is usually a #2 morse taper, with a center point and four spurs which are driven into the stock to be turned.

Fig. 9. **Cup or dead center**—The cup center is usually a #2 morse taper and fits into the tailstock spindle. It is sometimes called a "dead" center because it does not revolve, and does not drive the workpiece. The cup center has a thin circular rim around a concave end, which contains a center point. This center should be lubricated to reduce friction from the rotating stock.

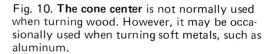

Fig. 10. **The cone center** is not normally used when turning wood. However, it may be occasionally used when turning soft metals, such as aluminum.

The ball-bearing cup center is commonly used to reduce friction during spindle turning. The cup center rotates during turning, and the ball bearings reduce noise and friction to a minimum.

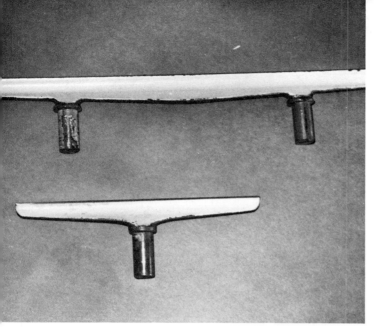

TOOL RESTS

Tool rests come in various shapes and sizes.

Fig. 11. The 12-inch tool rest is the most common, as it will accommodate most general lathe work.

The 24-inch tool rest is very useful when turning long stock. However, this tool rest requires two support bases.

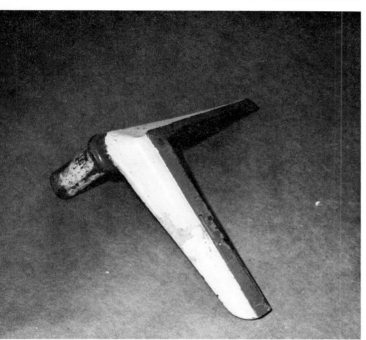

Fig. 12. The right angle tool rest is useful for faceplate work, as the face and edge can be turned without adjusting the tool rest and support base, once the initial adjustment has been made.

This tool rest is very useful, particularly when turning large bowls. Tool rests may also be custom-made for the operation.

Fig. 13. **Faceplates**—These are metal discs with a threaded hub which screws onto the headstock spindle. Stock is fastened to the faceplate by screws inserted through holes which have been drilled in the face plate. Faceplates are available in several diameters, according to the make of the lathe and the size of the stock to be turned.

Fig. 14. **Screw center faceplate**—This commonly a small faceplate, with a small screw center fastened to a tapered shank. It is a useful method for quickly mounting small faceplate turnings. It is not recommended for large pieces or high speeds.

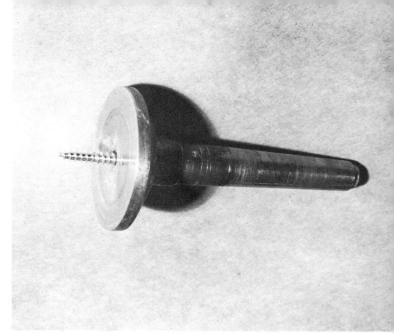

Fig. 15. **Geared chucks**—This chuck is fastened to a tapered shank and may be used in either the headstock or tailstock spindle. It is commonly used for holding drill bits for boring operations. It may also be used for holding small cylindrical stock for turning. The capacity of the chuck is usually a maximum of ½'' shank size.

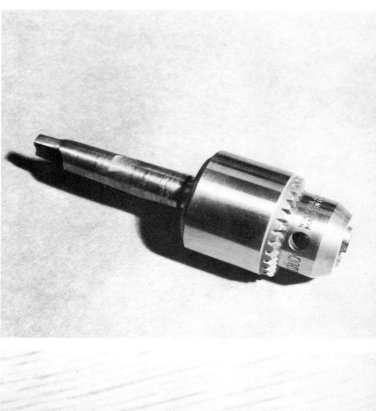

Fig. 16. **Drill pads**—These pads may be used with the geared chuck to perform boring operations. The geared chuck is placed in the headstock, and a drill bit is inserted into the chuck. The drill pad is held in the tailstock. The stock to be bored is placed against the drill pad, and is advanced into the drill bit by turning the tailstock handwheel in a clockwise direction.

Fig. 17. **Three-jaw self-centering chuck**—This is a chuck similar to those used on a metal lathe. It is useful for holding cylindrical stock for boring operations. The stock is automatically centered as the jaws tighten on the stock.

Fig. 18. **Sanding drums**—These are expandable rubber cylinders mounted on a tapered shank. A sanding sleeve is slid over the drum, and the nut is tightened, expanding the rubber cylinder and securely fastening the sleeve to the drum. Sanding drums are available in various sizes, and are useful for sanding contoured surfaces.

Fig. 19. **Arbor wheels**—These are two arbor washers mounted on a threaded arbor, which continues on to a tapered shank. The tapered shank fits into the spindle on the headstock. Various wheels, such as buffers, wire wheels, or grinding wheels may be installed. For safety, place a cone center in the tailstock spindle, and bring the point of the cone in contact with the center of the arbor. This will greatly decrease the possibility of the arbor coming out of the headstock during the grinding, buffing, or brushing operation.

7

Measuring and Layout Tools

Fig. 20. The rule—Either a steel rule or a tape may be used for laying out distances between centers.

It is good practice to make all measurements from one end of the stock. This minimizes errors which could be caused by an accumulation of small differences.

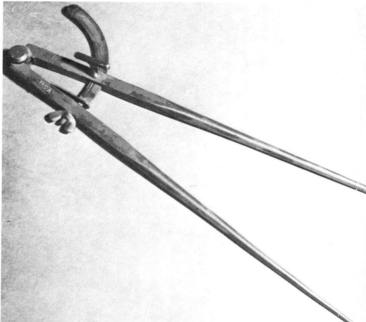

Fig. 21. Dividers—These have two sharp steel points, and are useful in stepping off measurements or making circles on faceplate work.

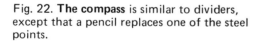

Fig. 22. The compass is similar to dividers, except that a pencil replaces one of the steel points.

It is useful for making circles, centering stock, or marking off distances.

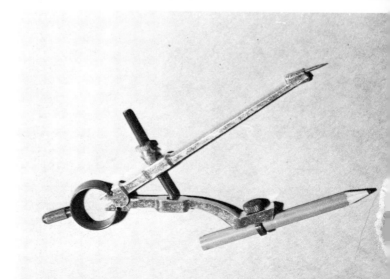

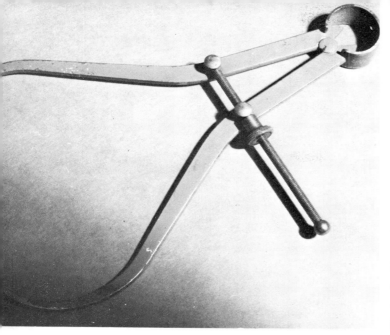

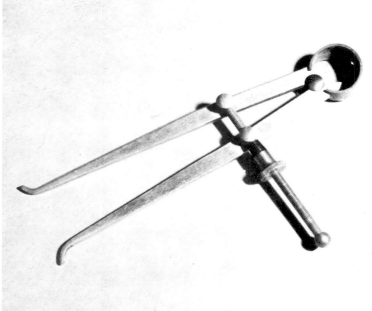

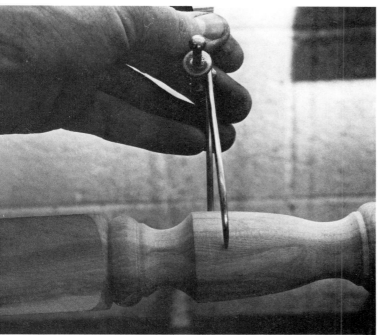

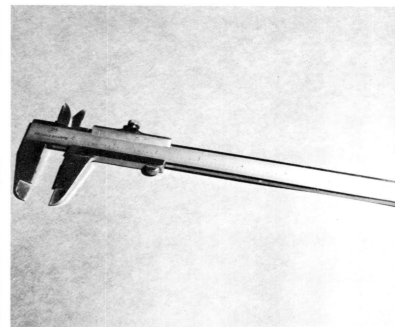

Fig. 23. **Calipers**—Outside calipers are used mainly to determine the diameter of a cylindrical object.

They are commonly used for checking diameters while the stock is rotating in the lathe. If this is the case, the points of the legs should be rounded, to prevent the calipers from catching in the work or marking the stock.

Fig. 24. When measuring diameters, always hold the calipers in a position at right angles to the stock.

The calipers should not be forced. If this is necessary, the stock is too large and needs to be reduced in diameter.

The calipers should lightly touch the stock as the legs pass over the work, if it is the correct size.

Fig. 25. Inside calipers are used to measure the inside diameters of holes or turnings such as goblets, bowls, and picture frames.

These should be used only when the stock is stopped.

Fig. 26. Vernier calipers are measuring tools commonly used in metal working. However, they are useful in wood turning, due to their accuracy and ease of setting.

Fig. 27. These calipers can be used for measuring outside diameters.

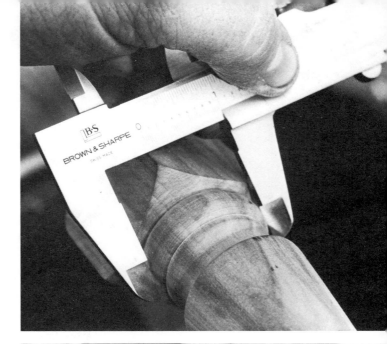

Fig. 28. Vernier calipers also can be used for measuring inside diameter, the depth of holes, or concave surfaces.

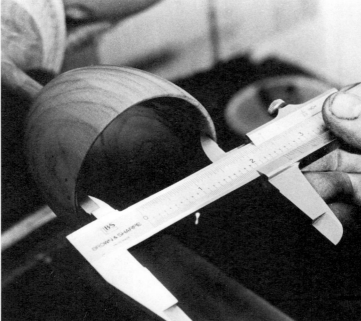

Fig. 29. Graduated step blocks are useful when a large amount of turning is to be done.

The blocks are graduated every 1/8'' and are turned to within .001 inch accuracy.

The calipers can be quickly and accurately set to the required diameter.

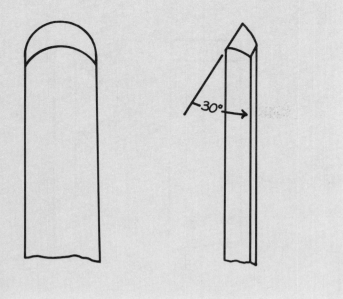

Lathe Tools

Fig. 30. **Gouges** are the most commonly used lathe tools, and are employed for roughing out stock and reducing stock to a cylindrical shape. They are also used for cutting coves or grooves on spindle turnings, or for making rough cuts or concave cuts on faceplate turnings. Gouges are beveled on the convex side of the tool. The bevel is approximately 30°, or twice as long as the thickness of the steel. Gouges have a rounded cutting end, extending well along the sides of the tool. They are commonly available in widths from ¼″ to 1″, with ½″ being the most common size.

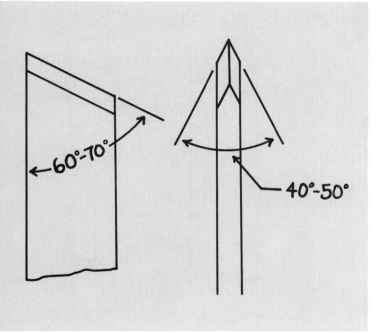

Fig. 31. **Skew chisels** are given that name because the cutting edge is at an angle to the side of the tool. The cutting edge is ground at an angle of 70° to one side of the chisel.

Normally, both sides of the cutting edge are bevelled, with the length of the bevel being approximately twice the thickness of the steel.

Skew chisels are used to make V cuts, beads, and tapers, and to smooth round shoulders or cylindrical stock. The skew may be used either as a cutting or scraping tool.

Some skew chisels are called right or left hand chisels. These skew chisels have only one side of the cutting edge bevelled, and are used only for scraping. Skew chisels are available in sizes from 1/8″ to 1½″. The most common are ½″ and 1″.

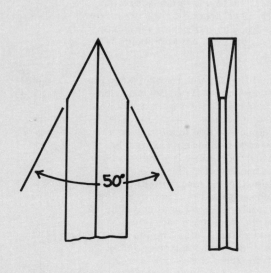

Fig. 32. **Parting tools** are used to make narrow recesses or grooves to a desired depth. The cut has flat sides and a square bottom. These tools are thicker at the center of the blade than at the edges. Their center thickness determines the width of the cut, which is normally 1/8″ or ¼″. The tapering from the center to the edge gives the tool clearance and helps prevent friction and head buildup from harming the tool or the stock. The parting tool makes a scraping cut, and is available in sizes from ½″ to 1″.

Fig. 33. **Roundnose** is a scraping tool commonly used in faceplate work. It can be used to make coves, grooves on spindle turnings, or concave areas such as in wooden bowls. The tool is generally used for rough turning. However, a sharp tool and a light cut is often utilized for producing a smooth finish. The roundnose has a rounded cutting edge, extending well along the sides of the tool. The bevel on the underside of the roundnose is 40°. Roundnose chisels are available in various sizes, the most common being 1/8'', ¼'', and ½''.

Fig. 34. **Diamond point** is a scraping tool used whenever its shape is needed to fit the shape of the stock. Its use is similar to that of right and left hand skew chisels. The cutting angle is 30° to the side of the tool, with the bevel 30° to the surface of the tool. A common size for the diamond point is ½''. Other sizes may be made by grinding skew or squarenose chisels to the shape of a diamond point.

Fig. 35. **Squarenose** is a scraping tool, usually used in smoothing flat or convex surfaces. As its name suggests, the tool is square across the front, with a 25° bevel ground on the underside of the cutting edge. The tool can be purchased in various widths, the most common being ½'' or ¾''.

Fig. 36. **The modified squarenose** is an adaptation of a squarenose chisel. This tool is ground at a 5° to 10° angle along the front edge, with a 25° bevel on the underside of the front edge. It is also ground along one side to a distance of 1½'' to 2''. The edge bevel is approximately 25°. The modified squarenose is ground in both a right- and left-hand model. The chisels are useful in roughing out the face plate turnings. The left-hand chisel is used to rough shape the outside of the stock, and the right-hand chisel is used to remove the stock from the concave area. Both of these chisels cut along the front as well as the side, thus removing stock quickly. A common width for these chisels is 1''.

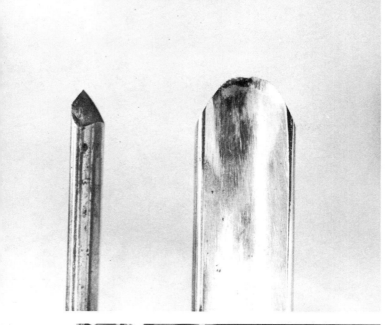

Sharpening Turning Chisels

Lathe tools are classified as cutting or scraping tools, and must be kept sharp and in good condition. High quality work can be obtained only through skilled use of sharp, properly ground tools.

Tools are ground to restore the tool to the correct cutting angle, or when the edges are nicked. After grinding, tools are whetted to make the cutting edge as sharp as possible. They may be whetted without grinding to restore sharpness.

Grinding is performed on a grinding wheel which has a true and even face. Always grind from the point of the bevel to the heel, as this will produce the smoothest edge.

Whetting is performed on oilstones, which are available in various grits. The usual procedure is to whet on the coarse grit, then finish whetting on the finest grit. Oil is normally used on the oilstone, as it acts as a lubricant and coolant, and removes particles of abrasives and metal from the surface of the oilstone.

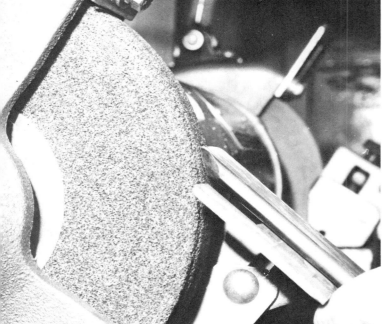

Fig. 37. Gouges are normally ground to a bevel of $30°$.

Check the bevel of the gouge. If the angle varies more than $2°$ or $3°$, the angle must be restored by grinding.

If the edge is nicked, it must be ground.

Fig. 38. Start the grinder, and bring the bevel in contact with the face of the wheel.

It is good practice to let the heel of the bevel contact the face of the wheel, then raise the handle of the gouge until the full bevel is in contact with the grinding wheel.

Fig. 39. With the full bevel in continuous contact with the wheel, roll the gouge over onto its side.

Now, rotate the gouge in the opposite direction, maintaining full contact with the face of the grinding wheel.

Repeat as above until the correct bevel has been restored and a sharp edge produced.

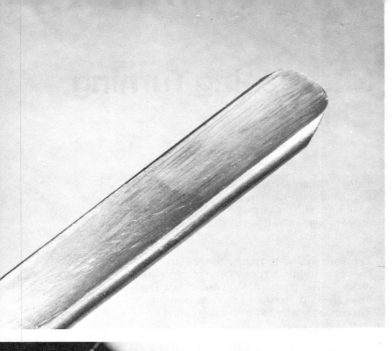

Fig. 40. Check the edge of the gouge carefully.

Shiny edges indicate a need for more grinding.

The edges should extend well back along the sides of the gouge.

The cutting edge should appear as an oval shape.

Small gouges are ground in a similar manner, although the small gouges have a more elliptical shape and a longer bevel.

Fig. 41. The gouge can also be sharpened against the flat side of a grinding wheel.

The gouge is supported by the tool rest and is rotated against the side of the wheel

Fig. 42. Pour a little lubricant on the oilstone.

To whet the gouge place it on the oilstone with the bevel flat against the surface of the oilstone.

Move the gouge in a circular motion, at the same time rotating the beveled edge from left to right.

Whet until a slight wire edge can be felt on the concave side of the gouge.

Fig. 43. Select a slipstone suitable for the size of gouge.

Place the round edge of the slipstone in the concave surface of the gouge, with at least 1/3 of the length of the stone protruding beyond the edge of the gouge.

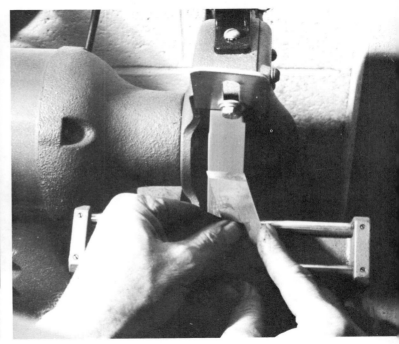

Fig. 44. Remove the wire edge by pulling the stone downward.

Be sure to keep the slipstone in contact with, and parallel to, the gouge.

Repeat as above until the wire edge is removed.

NOTE: It is not necessary to grind before you whet the gouge, but a gouge *must* be whetted after it has been ground.

Fig. 45. The skew must be correctly ground, particularly when making a shearing cut. A skew with more than one angle on the bevels will likely catch and run on the work.

For most work, the skew should be ground with a 20° to 25° angle on each bevel.

The side angle should be approximately 70°.

Fig. 46. To grind the bevel, start the machine and bring the bevel in contact with the face of the wheel.

Keep the cutting edge of the skew at a 90° angle to the side of the grinding wheel.

It is good practice to let the heel of the bevel contact the face of the wheel, then raise the handle of the skew until the full bevel contacts the grinding wheel.

Fig. 47. Hold the chisel in the position shown, and move it slowly back and forth across the face of the wheel.

The bevel must have a single straight or slightly concave face.

Fig. 48. When the bevel has been ground to the center of the chisel with the correct angle maintained, turn the chisel over and grind the other bevel.

Do not grind more than is necessary.

Check the edge frequently. Remember, shiny edges indicate a need for additional grinding.

Fig. 49. Grinding should cease when the metal starts to break away on the cutting edge, and the shiny spots have disappeared.

Fig. 50. Pour a little lubricant on the oilstone.

Place the bevel of the skew chisel flat against the surface of the oilstone.

Whet the chisel by moving the skew in a circular, or figure eight motion. *Keep the bevel flat against the oilstone.*

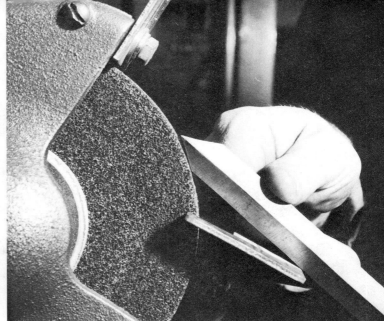

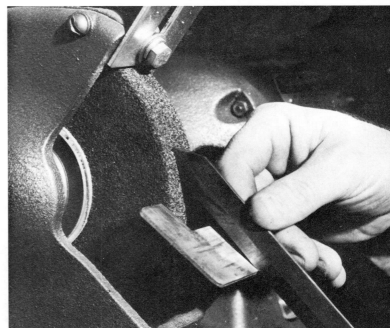

Fig. 51. When a wire edge appears on the cutting edge of the skew, turn it over and whet the other bevel.

Repeat the whetting operation until you are satisfied with the edge.

Fig. 52. The parting tool needs grinding frequently, as the cut is made by scraping action. Scraping cuts require a very sharp edge.

The parting tool should be ground at a 25° angle on each side.

Fig. 53. Start the grinder, and bring the heel of the bevel against the face of the grinding wheel.

Hold the cutting edge at a 90° angle to the side of the wheel.

Raise the handle of the parting tool until the full bevel is in contact with the wheel.

Fig. 54. Move the tool back and forth across the face of the wheel, exerting light pressure against the wheel.

Fig. 55. Grind the bevel until the cutting edge reaches the center line of the parting tool.

Turn the tool over and grind the other bevel.

The cutting edge must be at the center line, or the tool will not have proper clearance.

Examine the cutting edge.

Nicks or shiny places indicate the need for further grinding.

Fig. 56. To whet the parting tool, pour a little lubricating oil on the oilstone.

Grasping the tool firmly, place the full bevel in contact with the surface of the oilstone.

The tool must be perpendicular to the surface of the oilstone.

Fig. 57. Move the tool in a circular or figure eight motion.

Be sure the bevel is flat against the stone.

When a wire edge appears, turn the tool over and whet the other bevel.

The tool should be sharp when the wire edge disappears.

Fig. 58. The roundnose chisel is a scraping tool, and must be sharpened frequently.

The cutting edge should be somewhat elliptical in shape, with a 30° to 45° bevel on the underside of the cutting edge.

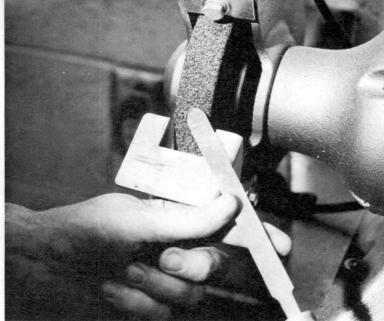

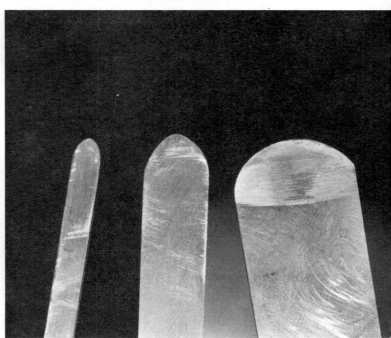

Fig. 59. Start the grinder, and bring the bevel in contact with the face of the wheel.

It is good practice to bring the heel of the bevel in contact with the wheel, then raise the handle until the full bevel is in contact with the face of the wheel.

Fig. 60. With the bevel in contact with the wheel, swing the handle slowly to the left, grinding from the center to the left side of the tool.

Repeat as above, only moving from right to left, grinding the other half of the bevel.

Fig. 61. Repeat the above step as necessary, always maintaining full bevel contact with the wheel.

Maintain the slightly elliptical shape of the cutting edge.

The cutting edge should be ground a good distance down both sides of the tool.

Fig. 62. Small roundnose chisels require a more elliptical cutting edge and a longer bevel.

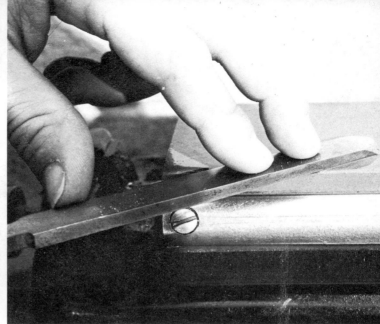

Fig. 63. Pour a little lubricating oil on the oilstone.

Hold the bevel flat against the surface of the stone.

Fig. 64. Roll the roundnose back and forth across the stone.

The bevel must be flat against the stone at all times.

When a wire edge appears on the flat surface, stop the whetting motion.

Fig. 65. Turn the roundnose over, and lay the tool flat on its top.

Move the tool back and forth or in a circular motion.

When the wire edge is removed, the tool should be sharp and ready for use.

Fig. 66. The squarenose chisel is also a scraping tool and must be kept very sharp.

The cutting edge is at right angles to the side of the tool, but the edge may be slightly convex.

The bevel on the underside of the cutting edge is ground at 25° - 30°.

Fig. 67. Start the grinder and bring the bevel in full contact with the face of the wheel.

Hold the cutting edge at a right angle to the side of the grinding wheel.

Exert light pressure, and move the tool back and forth across the face of the wheel.

Grind away slightly more metal at the edge of the chisel than at the center. This will produce a slightly convex cutting edge.

Fig. 68. Examine the edge frequently.

A shiny or nicked edge indicates the chisel needs further grinding.

Repeat the above sequence until the chisel is properly ground.

Fig. 69. Lubricate the oilstone.

Place the full bevel of the chisel flat on the surface of the oilstone.

While maintaining full bevel contact, move the chisel in a circular or figure eight motion.

When a wire edge appears, stop whetting the bevel.

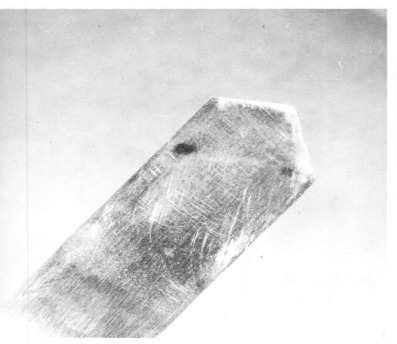

Fig. 70. Lay the top of the squarenose flat on the stone.

Move the tool back and forth or use a circular motion.

When the wire edge is removed, the tool should be sharp and ready for use.

Fig. 71. The diamond point is also a scraping tool and must be very sharp.

The diamond point is ground and beveled with two cutting edges at 30° angles to point of the tool.

Each angle has a beveled edge which is 30° to the top surface of the chisel.

Fig. 72. Hold the cutting edge at right angles to the side of the grinding wheel.

Bring the beveled edge in full contact with the face of the wheel.

Exert light pressure and move the tool back and forth across the wheel.

Fig. 73. Examine the edge frequently.

Need for further grinding is indicated by a shiny or nicked edge.

Continue grinding until you are satisfied with the edge.

Lay the top of the diamond point flat on the stone and hone in the usual manner.

NOTE: The point of the chisel must be at an equal distance from both sides of the tool.

A Controversy: Which Method, Cutting or Scraping?

A dilemma which often faces the instructor or student is which method to use—cutting or scraping. The answer is up to the individual. However, the following discussion will present the strengths and weaknesses of each method.

The Cutting Method

The cutting method has been the accepted method of turning for many generations. The techniques were handed down from father to son, and were jealously guarded by the craftsman. This method is the oldest method used. It is the fastest and cleanest method of turning. However, it can be learned only with much practice and patience on the part of the learner. The basic tools used in cutting are the skew and the gouge. All flat, tapered, or convex surfaces are rounded and smoothed with the shearing cut made by the skew chisel. Coves, circular grooves, and even beads are made with the shearing cut made by a gouge. Most of the basic spindle turnings were made with these two chisels.

The professional woodturner employs the cutting method wherever possible. The personal satisfaction and sense of achievement derived from a mastering of the cutting method is enjoyed only by a few master woodturners. This goal is something the beginner might set for himself.

The Scraping Method

The scraping method is used extensively in the patternmaking trade. It is a newer method than cutting, developed by the foundry industry to produce accurate patterns for mold making. The skew is also a basic tool for scraping. However, it is usually sharpened with one bevel, and used as a right- and left-hand tool. The diamond point and squarenose chisels are also used. All flat, tapered, or convex cuts are made with the skew, squarenose, or diamond point chisels. All coves or circular grooves are made with the roundnose chisel.

The scraping method may be quickly and easily learned. This method is not as fast as cutting and the work will require more sanding. It does produce the most accurate turnings, as the amount of material removed can be precisely controlled. The worker who does not turn regularly will find that scraping will produce satisfactory results.

As turning is not a major part of cabinetmaking, the scraping method is probably best for those who wish to turn a few articles for their own use. The results are satisfactory and finished turnings may be produced with less practice or loss of stock.

In summary, the choice is left up to the individual. Both methods may be used in industry, in training institutions, or by the home craftsman. However, to become a professional turner, with the satisfaction derived from mastery of a difficult skill, it is necessary to learn the art of cutting.

by E. N. Pearson

Stock Selection and Preparation for Turning

Stock for lathe work must be good quality material, free from defects such as shake, checks, or dead knots. Unsound stock is apt to come apart during the turning operation, with resulting hazards to machine, operator, and bystanders.

Glued-up stock must be carefully assembled, with quality craftsmanship in fitting and assembly. Only high quality adhesives should be used, with adequate setting time for the adhesive before the stock is turned. Glued-up stock is always turned at slower speeds than solid stock, because of the possibility of failure of a glue joint.

Fig. 74. The material shown here is not suitable for lathe work. Remove all knots, splits, and cracks, or select another piece.

Fig. 75. Stock for spindle turning should be at least cut to square dimensions. This is all that is necessary for stock up to 2½" square.

For stock with square dimensions larger than 2½", lay out the diagonals and find the center point.

Set a compass at a radius equal to ½ the square of the stock.

Using the center point as the pivot, scribe a circle on the end of the stock.

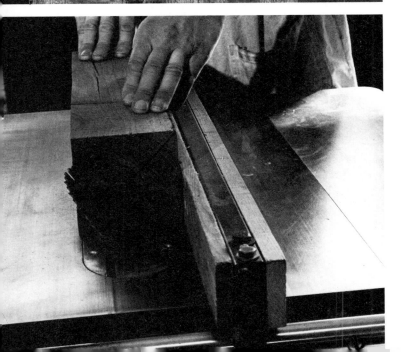

Fig. 76. Set the circular saw at an angle of 45°.

Position the stock so the waste piece will be on the outside of the blade.

Cut off the corners of the stock, taking care to cut in the waste part of the stock.

Fig. 77. The approximate octagonal shape will lessen machine vibration and will allow you to start turning at a higher speed and complete the turning in less time.

Fig. 78. Faceplate turning also requires the stock to be cut to rough shape.

Select the stock and plane one side flat and smooth.

Fig. 79. Lay out and mark the desired circle, allowing at least ¼'' in diameter for trueing up the stock.

Fig. 80. Band saw the stock to rough shape, always cutting in the waste material.

The stock is now ready for mounting on a faceplate.

It is often necessary to find the center point on an irregularly shaped piece of stock. Although the center point can be found by trial and error, the process can be time-consuming. A bit of applied geometry will solve the problem. When a right triangle is placed inside a circle, one half the hypotenuse will be the center point of the circle.

The following method is quick and accurate:

Fig. 81. Place a square on the stock and mark the three points where the square touches the edge of the stock.

Fig. 82. Draw a line from point *one* to point *three*.

This line represents the hypotenuse of the triangle.

Fig. 83. Measure the length of the hypotenuse.

Divide the length by two, and place a mark at the center of the hypotenuse.

The mark of the center point of the hypotenuse will be the center point of the stock.

Fig. 84. Using the center point as a pivot point, set the compass to a distance equal to the shortest distance from the center point to edge of the stock.

Mark a circle with the compass.

Fig. 85. The marked stock may look something like this.

Fig. 86. Use a band saw, and cut the stock to its rough size.

Turning Stock Between Centers: Centering and Mounting the Stock

One of the first steps in spindle turning is centering the stock. This must be performed accurately to allow the maximum size of cylinder to be turned from the stock. Stock that is not properly centered will vibrate excessively since it is out of balance, and may fly from the lathe with the possibility of injury to the operator or a bystander.

For certain operations, such as turning pieces with rectangular sections, or built-up turnings, it is important that the stock be perfectly centered. Otherwise, the turning will not have a symmetrical appearance.

In general, proceed as follows:

Fig. 87. Select the stock, and cut it to rough dimensions, allowing an extra inch in length and 1/8 to ¼ inch thicker and wider than the finished dimensions.

However, if the turning has rectangular parts, it is usually cut and jointed to the exact dimensions with regard to thickness and width.

Square the ends, and mark the center, using one of the following methods.

Fig. 88. Locate the center by the use of diagonal lines.

Using a pencil and straightedge, draw lines diagonally across the ends of the stock. The lines will intersect at the center of the piece.

This is the best method to use with square or rectangular stock.

Fig. 89. To locate the center of an irregularly shaped block, set the dividers at a distance 1/8 to ¼" greater than one half the width or thickness of the block.

Draw lines on the end of the stock, using each surface as the guide.

Draw diagonals within the area enclosed by the lines. The intersection of the lines indicates the center of the stock.

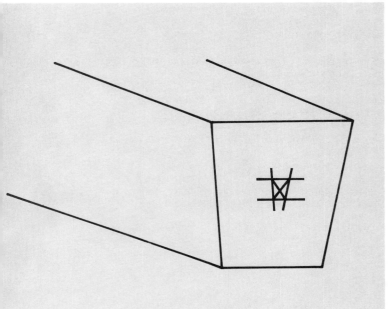

Fig. 90. Select one end of the stock for the spur center.

Cut a saw kerf along the diagonal lines. Make the kerf 1/8 inch deep.

Fig. 91. Place the stock on a solid surface.

Center punch a hole at the exact center of the stock. (The hole should be 1/16 to 3/32 inch in diameter.)

Do this on each end of the piece.

Fig. 92. Using a wooden mallet (to prevent damage to the spur center), drive the spur center into the stock.

Be sure the center is in the hole, and that the spurs enter the saw kerfs.

Fig. 93. Place some lubricating material on the end of the stock or in the cup center.

Wax, soap, tallow, or oil all may be used as a lubricant, but oil will penetrate the wood and possibly stain the stock.

Loosen the tailstock spindle clamp, and turn the spindle until it protrudes about one inch from the tailstock.

Fig. 94. Place the spur center in the spindle of the headstock.

Do not loosen the spur center from the stock.

Fig. 95. Loosen the tailstock clamp, and move the tailstock up to the stock.

Tighten the tailstock clamp.

Turn the spindle feed handwheel, and insert the point of the cup center into the center hole in the stock.

Fig. 96. Continue turning until the cup center is securely seated into the wood.

Turn the handwheel back about 1/8 of a turn. This will decrease the pressure of the cup center, and will help prevent excess friction at the point of contact.

Fig. 97. Lock the spindle clamp handle.

Turn the stock by hand, being sure it turns freely, but without end play.

Fig. 98. Loosen the tool rest base clamp, and move the tool rest into a position parallel to the stock, and 1/8'' away from every corner of the stock.

Rotate the stock by hand, and check the setting.

Lock the tool rest base clamp.

Fig. 99. Loosen the tool rest clamp and raise or lower the tool rest until it is in a position about 1/8'' above the center of the stock.

Lock the tool rest clamp.

Rotate the stock by hand, and check the setting with regard to all four corners of the stock.

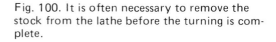

Fig. 100. It is often necessary to remove the stock from the lathe before the turning is complete.

Mark the end of the stock with reference to the file mark on the spur center.

When replacing the stock, line up the mark on the stock with the file mark on the spur center.

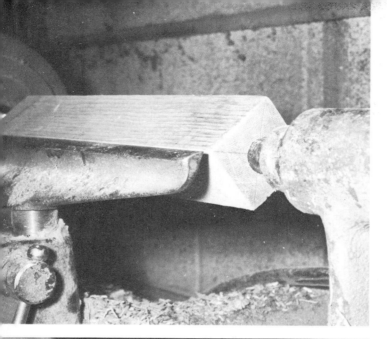

Turning Stock Between Centers: Gouge-Turning a Cylinder

Fig. 101. Center the stock in the lathe.

The tool rest should be about 1/8" from the stock.

Fig. 102. Using the gouge, round off one end of the stock.

Cut only in the waste part of the stock.

Fig. 103. Turn the stock until the flat part showing the largest shoulder appears.

Hold the pencil against the point where the flat area is tangent to the shoulder.

Run a line around the stock.

This line indicates the diameter you must cut to bring the stock into a cylindrical shape.

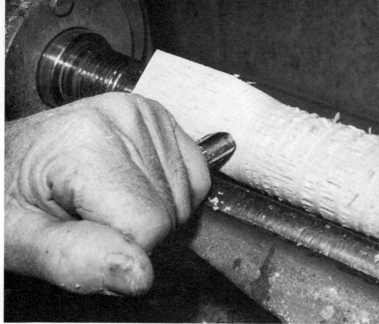

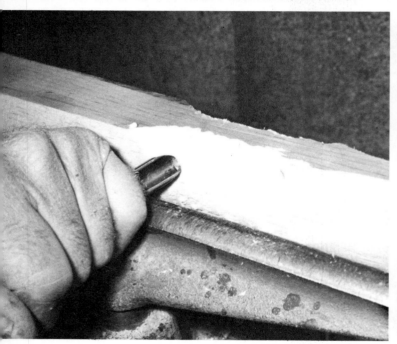

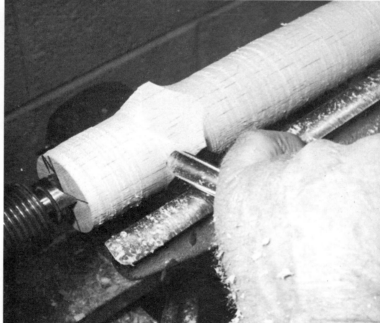

Fig. 104. Start the lathe, and begin a series of light shearing cuts.

Fig. 105. Each cut should be 1½" to 2" in length, and, for beginners, should be light. As you progress and become more confident and skilled, the cuts will become heavier.

Fig. 106. Stop about 1½" to 2" from the end of the stock.

Fig. 107. Roll the gouge over and begin cutting at the point where the last cut stopped.

Continue to the end of the stock.

Repeat as shown, until the work is turned to a cylinder.

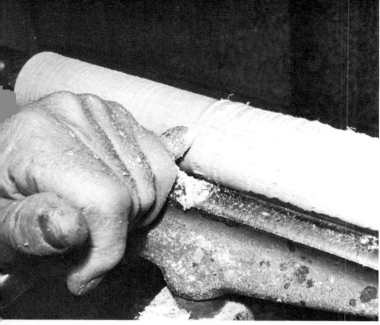

Fig. 108. Hold the gouge in a shearing position.

Start from the left end of the stock.

Make a continuous cut the full length of the stock.

Fig. 109. As soon as the stock becomes a cylinder, increase the speed of the lathe (the speed is determined by the diameter of the cylinder).

Make a final shearing cut.

At this point, the stock is in shape for basic layout.

Smoothing a Cylinder

Fig. 110. Turn the cylinder to rough size.

Position the tool rest to a point about 1/8" above the center of the stock.

Hold the chisel at an angle 25° to 30° to the surface of the stock, with the bevel resting on the surface of the stock.

Fig. 111. Hold the skew in a shearing position, point above the stock, with the stock contacting the lower half of the skew.

The chisel position and angle are reversed when cutting the opposite direction.

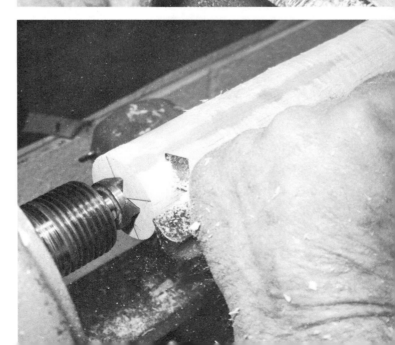

Fig. 112. The first cut, made from right to left, smooths a section one to two inches wide.

This is necessary to prevent the possibility of the skew catching the shoulder of the stock.

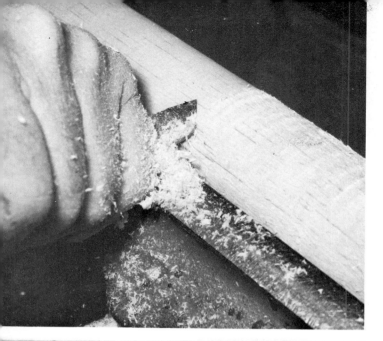

Fig. 113. Hold the skew securely and take a light cut the length of the cylinder.

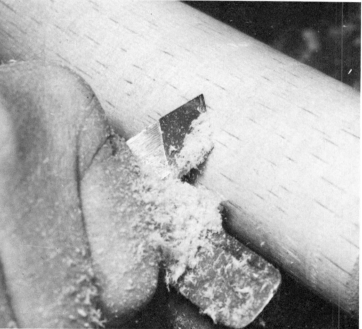

Fig. 114. It may be necessary to make two or three cuts to produce the desired surface.

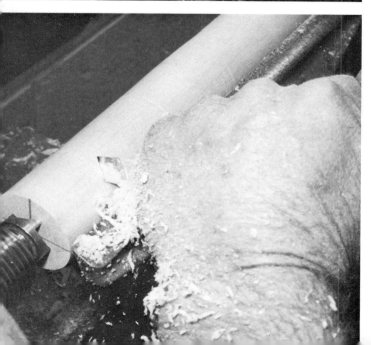

Fig. 115. The cylinder may be smoothed by cutting from left to right or right to left. It is a matter of preference.

The correct cutting action will produce a shaving rather than sawdust.

Fig. 116. The cylinder may also be smoothed with a skew in scraping position.

Fig. 117. Check the cylinder for flatness.

If necessary, remove material until the cylinder is flat and smooth.

Sand to final finish.

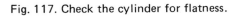

Turning Between Centers: Using the Parting Tool for Cutting to Length

The parting tool is used to produce cuts with straight sides. This is commonly done when cutting to length, cutting to depth, squaring shoulders, or cutting grooves with square sides.

When used properly, the parting tool cuts with a shearing type of action. This is accomplished by bringing the tool in contact with the stock, then lowering the handle 5° to 10° and moving the tool into the stock. To maintain the correct cutting angle, the handle must be raised as the tool cuts into the cylinder, because of the continuous change in stock diameter.

The shearing type cut which can be made with the parting tool is still basically a scraping cut. A very sharp edge must therefore be maintained on the tool. Caution must also be used to prevent burning the end of the parting tool, owing to the extreme heat built up during the cutting process.

Fig. 118. Mount the stock in the lathe, with the tool rest at, or slightly below, center.

Rough-turn the stock to its approximate diameter.

Increasing the lathe speed, make a final smoothing cut over the full length of the cylinder.

Fig. 119. Stop the lathe.

Move the tool rest to within 1/8" of the cylinder.

Locate and mark a point indicating one end of the turning.

Mark the line around the cylinder.

Fig. 120. Lay out the length of the turning measuring from the previous mark.

Mark the line around the cylinder.

Fig. 121. The left and right hand lines represent the finished length of the turning.

Fig. 122. Be sure the parting tool is sharpened to a keen edge. If necessary, grind the tool before whetting.

Start the lathe.

Position the parting tool so the cut will be in the *waste stock.*

Lower the handle 5° to 10° below the tool rest.

Move the tool forward until it contacts the moving cylinder.

Raise the handle as the tool cuts into the stock, at the same time pushing the tool forward.

Fig. 123. The parting tool must be held at a 90° angle to the work.

Part of the line should be left on the stock; otherwise the length will be undersized.

If the end is to be cut smooth, start the cut at least 1/16 inch away from the line, and finish smoothing the end with a skew chisel.

Fig. 124. Repeat at the other end of the cylinder.

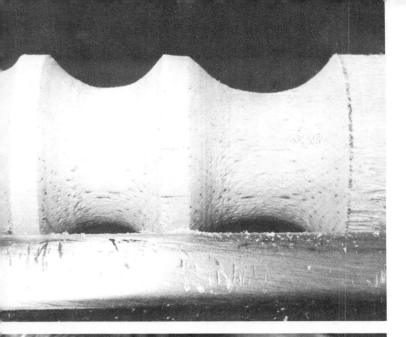

Spindle Turning: Cutting Coves, Scraping Method

Coves may be made either by cutting or scraping.

Coves cut by the cutting method are smoother than those done by the scraping method and can be made in less time. However, much practice is required.

The scraping method is more suitable for the beginner and is more accurate than cutting, but requires more time to make the cove. Also, more sanding is required.

Fig. 125. # 1. Cove was made using the cutting method. (See sequence "Turning Stock Between Centers: Using a Gouge to Make Coves or Grooves," page 46.)

2. Cove was made by the scraping method, using a roundnose chisel.

Fig. 126. Lay out the desired width of the coves.

Fig. 127. Use the point of the skew chisel and cut a V-groove on the inside of the line.

The V-groove points to the bottom, center point of the cove.

Cut a V-groove on both sides of the cove.

Do not remove the line.

Fig. 128. Select a sharp roundnose chisel, the width of which is at least 1/8" less than the width of the cove.

Place the chisel flat on the tool rest, bevel side down, and at 90° to the stock.

Feed the roundnose straight into the center of the cove.

Continue to the desired depth.

Fig. 129. Position the roundnose chisel so the chisel contacts the shoulder of the cove just below the surface of the stock.

Cut from the shoulder down to the center of the cove.

Fig. 130. Repeat the above step on the other shoulder of the cove.

Always cut from the shoulder down to the center of the cove. This will minimize tearing out the wood fibers.

Fig. 131. Small coves can be made by using small roundnose chisels.

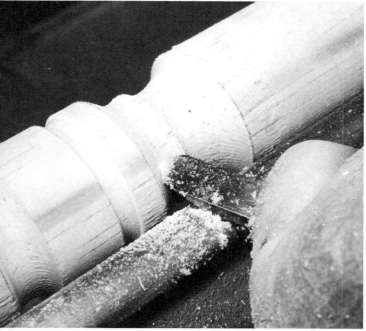

Fig. 132. Large coves are made in a manner similar to that shown here. The only difference is that more cuts are necessary.

Fig. 133. These are excellent examples of coves cut using the scraping method.

Spindle Turning: Cutting Beads, Scraping Method

Beads may be formed either by the cutting or the scraping method. Both methods require a sharp skew chisel, properly ground.

Beads made by the cutting method are smoother and can be completed in a minimum of time. However, this method requires much practice.

The scraping method may be more suitable for the beginner. It is more accurate than cutting, but requires more time to complete the bead. Also, more sanding is required.

Fig. 134. #1. Bead was made using the cutting method. (See "Turning Between Centers: Making Beads with Skew Chisel, Cutting Method," page 50.)

#2 Bead was formed by the scraping method.

Fig. 135. Now—how it is done:

Lay out the beads.

Use the point of the skew chisel, and cut a V-groove at both sides of the bead.

Fig. 136. Lay the skew chisel flat on the tool rest.

The point should point toward the bottom of the V-groove.

This necessitates that the skew chisel be held at an angle to the stock.

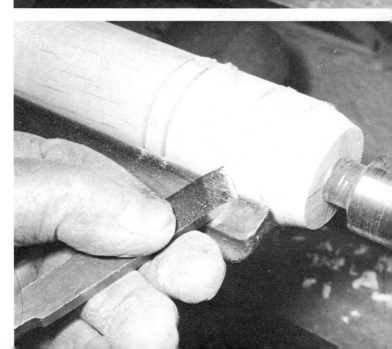

Fig. 137. Feed the point of the skew into the V-grooves, at the same time moving the handle of the chisel toward the center of the bead.

Fig. 138. Reversing the position of the skew, form the other side of the bead.

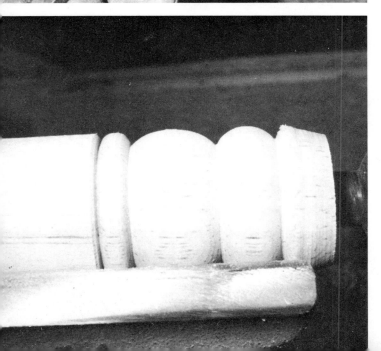

Fig. 139. Repeat the above procedure until the bead has been formed to your satisfaction.

It may be necessary to deepen the V-groove as the bead is being formed.

Turning Stock Between Centers: Using a Gouge to Make Coves or Grooves

A common use for the gouge is to make coves or grooves. A concave cut which is elliptical in shape is called a cove; one which is circular in shape is called a groove. Both cuts are commonly used when turning between centers, their main use to allow a change in dimension from diameters of various sizes. The transition from large to small, or small to large, diameters is facilitated by their use. However, the cove is usually preferred, because of its more pleasing appearance and its application to good design.

Using a gouge correctly primarily requires a knowledge of the tool, and of its use and practice. Carefully follow the instructional sequence and, with a reasonable amount of practice, you can become proficient in cutting grooves or coves with a gouge.

For this operation to be successful, the gouge must be correctly ground and whetted to a keen edge.

Fig. 140. Mount the stock in the lathe and turn it to rough size.

Make one full-length shearing cut with the gouge.

Lay out the widths of the coves or beads.

Transfer the layout dimensions completely around the cylinder.

Fig. 141. Adjust the tool rest to a position even with the center of the stock, and about 1/8 inch away from the stock.

Using the skew, make an angle cut about 1/8 inch deep which points toward the center of the cove.

Fig. 142. Make a similar cut on the other side of the cove.

These cuts form a shoulder against which the gouge is positioned.

This shoulder helps keep the gouge in position, and prevents it from running down the stock.

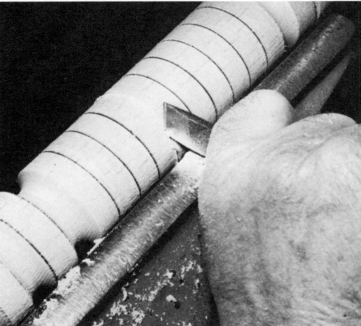

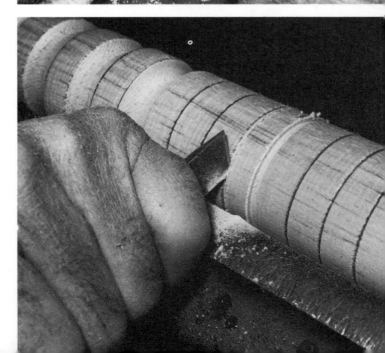

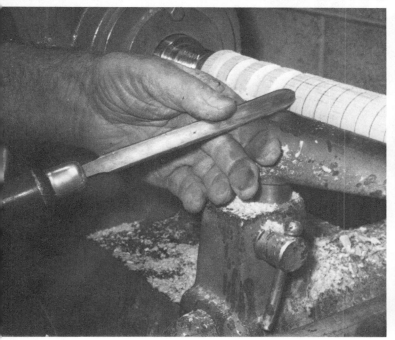

Fig. 143. The gouge is held at an angle of 25°
to 30° to the stock.

Fig. 144. The handle of the gouge is 10° to 15°
below the tool rest.

Start the machine, and increase the speed to the
desired rpm.

Lay the gouge on its side, and establish the
correct angle.

Fig. 145. Hold the gouge at an angle of 25°
to 30° to the stock, with the handle 10° to
15° below the tool rest.

Bring the point of the lip into the cut made
with the skew.

Raise the handle slowly, causing the lip to cut
deeper into the stock at the same time.

Roll the gouge over until a small groove is cut
into the cylinder.

Fig. 146. Proceed as in previous step, but cut
on the left side of the cove.

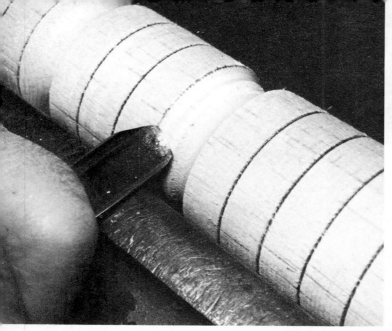

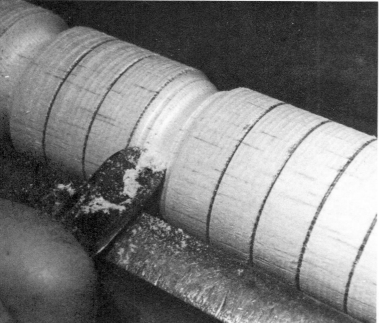

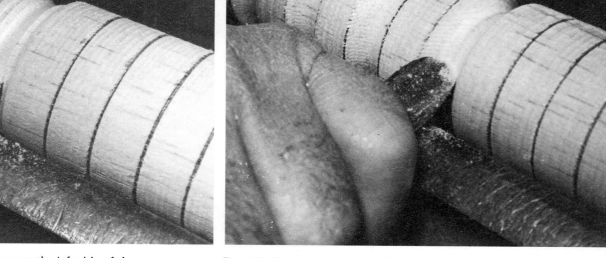

Fig. 147. Keep the gouge on the left side of the cut.

Using a shearing cut, remove the center of the cove.

Fig. 148. This series of cuts will cut the cove to rough dimension.

Fig. 149. Starting at one side of the cove, lay the gouge on its side, and hold it at the correct angles.

Push the gouge forward, raising the handle slightly, and keep the bevel of the gouge in contact with the shoulder of the cove.

The bevel in contact with the shoulder will control the depth of cut.

Fig. 150. As the gouge is moved forward, roll the tool until it is in flat position.

Caution: Do not cut beyond the center of the cove or groove.

Repeat as above, working from the other side of the cut. This requires reversing the gouge and re-establishing the correct angles.

Fig. 151. Continue working from the left side of the cove or groove, making one cut and then reversing to the right side for the alternate cut. Keep the following points in mind at all times:

1. In starting the cut, always bring the bevel of the gouge into contact with the shoulder of the cut *before* the lip of the gouge contacts the stock.

2. After the width of the cut has been established, always start the cuts just below the top edge of the groove or cove.

3. *Practice.*

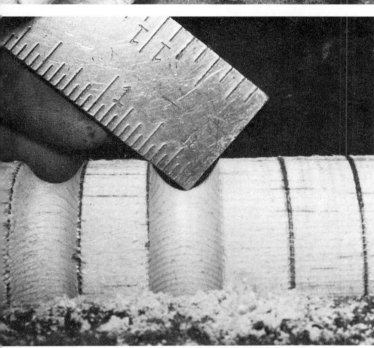

Fig. 152. Sometimes it is necessary to check a groove for roundness. One way is to place a square into the groove. If the square touches at three points the groove is round.

As you practice cutting grooves or coves, your eye will become accustomed to judging the accuracy of the cut. It will help if you watch the back of the cut to see the shape the gouge is forming.

You may want to check the depth of the cuts by the use of calipers. Usually this is not necessary as the experienced worker can estimate the depth needed. However, if calipers are used, stop the lathe to check the depth. Otherwise, the calipers may leave a mark on the surface of the cut.

Fig. 153. Practice making coves and grooves until you feel confident.

With continuing practice you will become an expert.

Turning Between Centers: Making Beads with Skew Chisel, Cutting Method

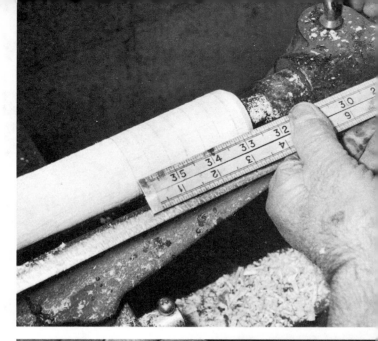

The cutting method is the fastest and cleanest method of turning beads, but it is difficult to learn and requires much practice. The expert wood turner uses the cutting method almost exclusively, as the cuts can be made quickly and smoothly. In fact, the cutting method produces surfaces so smooth that little or no sanding is required. The cutting method is difficult to learn, but consistent practice and patience, and following correct procedures, will enable the beginner to learn this method in a short time, and thus experience the satisfaction of performing in a professional manner.

The following sequence must be carefully studied, with attention paid to all the details. After studying the sequence, select a piece of softwood and practice the operation.

Fig. 154. Turn the stock to the rough diameter and mark the ends of the turning.

Set the tool rest about 1/8'' from the stock, slightly above center.

Mark the width of the beads, and continue the lines around the cylinder.

Fig. 155. Start the lathe, adjusting the speed to the desired rpm.

For large beads, use a pencil and draw a light line around the cylinder at the center of the bead. For beads less than ½ inch in width, this may not be necessary.

Examine the skew chisel to make sure it has the correct bevel and has been whetted to a keen edge.

Lay the skew chisel on its back with the point in line with the mark on the stock.

Be sure the skew is at 90° from the surface of the stock, with the bevel in vertical position.

Push the skew forward into the stock, cutting a sharp V-groove between the two beads. The groove should be approximately 1/8'' deep.

Fig. 156. Make the V-groove on both sides of the bead.

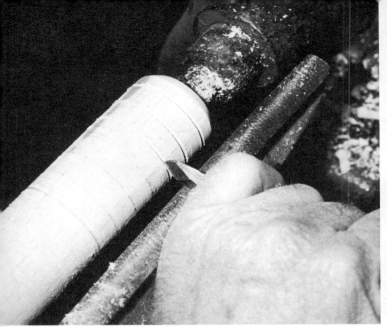

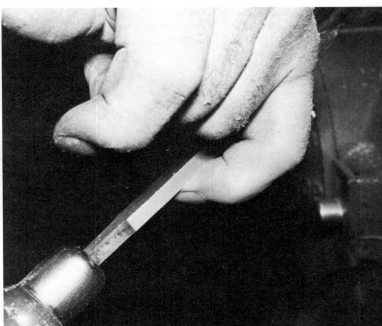

Fig. 157. If several beads are to be cut, make all the V-grooves at the same time.

Fig. 158. For cutting a bead, the skew should be held at an angle of 25° to 30° to the stock.

Fig. 159. The handle of the skew should be dropped until the angle is from 5° to 10° below the tool rest.

Fig. 160. Grasp the skew firmly, with the little finger under the skew and against the tool rest.

Fig. 161. The angle of the skew is about 45°
from vertical.

Push the skew forward until the lower half of
the skew contacts the surface of the cylinder at
the center of the bead.

The bevel of the skew should be flat against the
cylinder, without the edge cutting into the
stock.

Slightly raise the handle of the skew and begin
the cut.

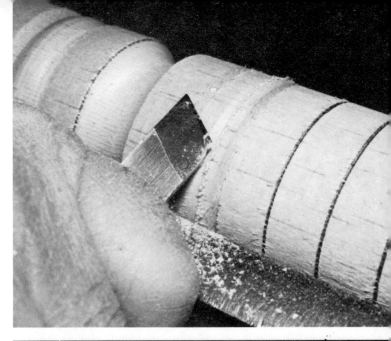

Fig. 162. As the cut progresses, roll the chisel
slowly over in the direction in which you are
cutting.

Fig. 163. As the skew is rolled, the handle is
raised slightly and the skew pushed forward.
This is done in one continuous motion.

Fig. 164. The cut is finished with the skew in vertical position.

The heel of the skew may be pushed in to start another V-groove if the intersection between the beads needs to be deeper.

Fig. 165. The left half of the bead is cut exactly as shown in pictures 8 through 11, except that the angles must be reversed.

Contact the center of the bead.

Fig. 166. Roll the skew, moving forward and over the bead.

Fig. 167. With proper chisel action, the bead will be formed perfectly.

Fig. 168. The results will be pleasing and satisfying.

Finish the cut with the skew in vertical position.

Fig. 169. A series of well-formed beads come as a result of practice, patience, and attention to detail.

Using the cutting method to turn a bead with a skew is a most satisfying experience. The beginning wood turner will experience some difficulty, but this will be overcome with practice and attention to details.

Most errors in this operation can be attributed to:

1. An improperly ground skew chisel, with an incorrect cutting angle

2. A dull chisel

3. A tool rest which is too low

4. Holding the tool at an incorrect angle to the stock

CAUTION: Practice first on softwood, then graduate to hardwood and turn like a professional.

Cutting V-Grooves

Fig. 170. Lay out the width of the V-groove.

Use the point of the skew and cut a small V-groove.

Cut to about ¾ of the depth required.

Changing the angle of skew will widen the V-groove and allow the skew to cut deeper.

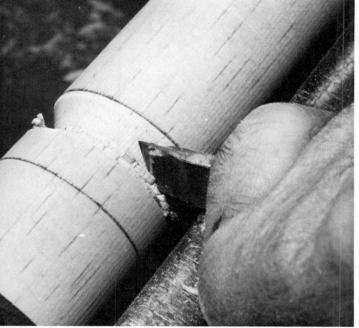

Fig. 171. Hold the skew in cutting position and remove part of the shoulder.

Continue removing material until the width of the groove has been reached.

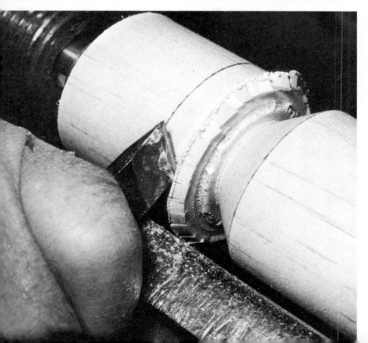

Fig. 172. Reversing the position of the skew, cut the left shoulder.

Notice the material being removed in small pieces.

Fig. 173. Continue cutting until the V-groove reaches its final shape.

Fig. 174. A finished V-groove requires little or no sanding.

Cutting and Smoothing Shoulders

Fig. 175. A shoulder cut made with a parting tool is often rough, and may need to be smoothed.

Fig. 176. Hold the skew chisel so the point will remove about 1/32" of material.

Fig. 177. The point of the skew does the cutting. The bevel on the skew rides along the shoulder, acting as a guide and producing a flat smooth shoulder.

Fig. 178. A finished shoulder, as shown here, is smooth and flat, requiring little sanding.

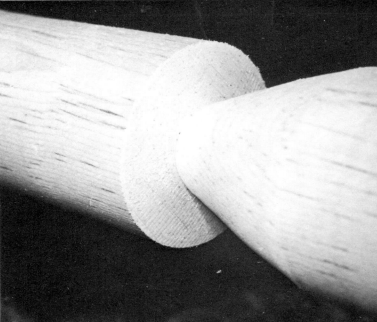

Spindle Turning: Cutting a Taper

Fig. 179. Using a gouge, rough turn the stock to its approximate diameter.

Then, using a parting tool and calipers, cut to the desired diameter for the large end of the taper.

Fig. 180. Cut the diameter of the small end of the taper.

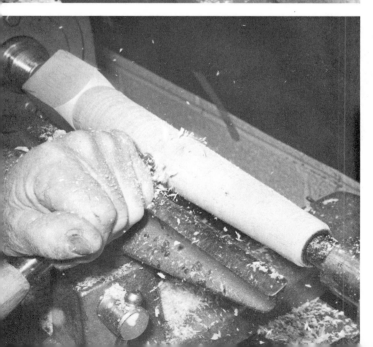

Fig. 181. Rough out the taper. A ½-inch gouge works well for this step.

Fig. 182. The roughed-out taper should be to rough size. Care must be taken to make sure the taper is not undersize at any point.

Fig. 183. Check the taper for flatness.

If necessary, remove excess material.

Fig. 184. Using a shearing cut, smooth the taper.

Fig. 185. The taper may also be smoothed by using a wide skew chisel in a scraping position.

Fig. 186. Check carefully to be sure the taper is flat.

Fig. 187. A final sanding will produce a finished taper.

by E. N. Pearson

Turning Between Centers: Turnings with Rectangular Sections

In furniture construction, it is often necessary to turn parts which have areas composed of rectangular sections. These sections are common in legs on tables, chairs, and other types of furniture. Turnings of this type require careful layout, and particular attention must be paid to centering the stock in the lathe. The part to be cut—usually composed of coves, beads, rounds, and tapers—is then turned in the usual manner. However, particular attention must be given when turning the curved shoulder on the rectangular section. This requires a shearing cut with the skew chisel to give the best appearance. Practice may be necessary before attempting this cut on the finished part.

Fig. 188. Legs such as these commonly contain rectangular sections which are used in joining the leg to other parts of the chair.

Fig. 189. Cut and joint the stock to the size of the largest rectangular section. In most cases the dimensions are the same along the full length of the stock.

Carefully lay out the rectangular sections.

Fig. 190. Mark the diagonals on each end of the stock.

They must be precise, with the intersections at the exact center of the stock. Otherwise the piece will lack a balanced appearance.

Fig. 191. Mount the stock in the lathe.

Check tool rest height and clearance.

Make the relocating mark on the end next to the spur center.

Fig. 192. Mark and cut the shoulders on the rectangular sections.

Lay the skew with the point of the skew next to the tool rest.

Start the lathe, feeding the skew into the stock until it reaches the point where it is cutting all around the stock.

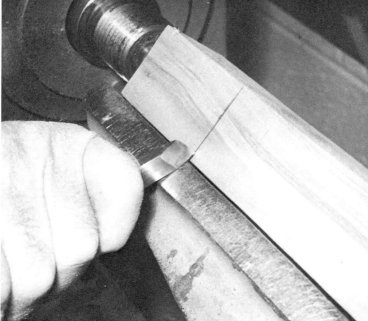

Fig. 193. Change the angle of the skew, cutting on the left and right sides of the first cut. This will form a V-cut around the stock.

Fig. 194. Position the skew at an angle to the work, with the point of the skew above the edge of the rotating stock.

The point must be above the corner of the stock. Otherwise the point will grab and tear a piece out of the rectangular section.

Fig. 195. Using a shearing cut, turn the curved part of the shoulder.

For a deep cut it may be necessary to remove some of the waste stock before the final cut can be made.

Fig. 196. Rough out the cylindrical parts of the turning.

Using a gouge, make shearing cuts.

Fig. 197. Cutting next to the shoulder requires that the angle of the gouge be reversed.

Do not touch the shoulder.

Fig. 198. Lay out and cut the beads.

In this sequence use the skew and make a shearing cut.

Fig. 199. For further information, refer to the sequence "Turning Between Centers: Making Beads with Skew Chisel, Cutting Method," page 50.

The beads may also be made by scraping, but more sanding will be required.

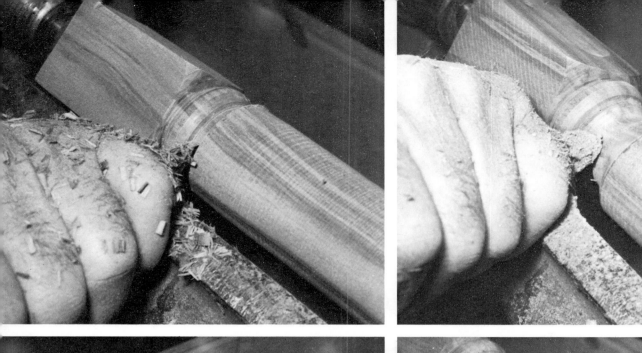

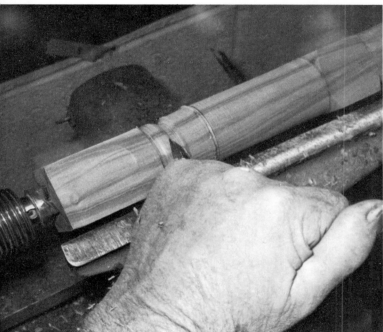

Fig. 200. If a shoulder is required next to a bead use the parting tool.

Fig. 201. The skew chisel is used to cut a V-groove at the point where the cove will meet the shoulder.

Fig. 202. The cove may be cut with a gouge or scraped with a roundnose chisel.

Fig. 203. The beads are cut before the coves are made.

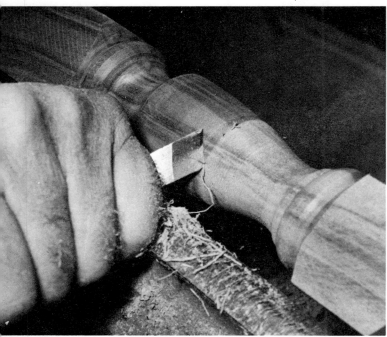

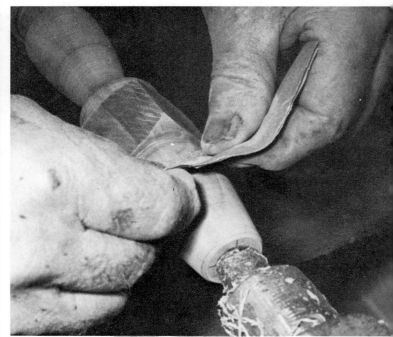

Fig. 204. All parts are roughed out.

Fig. 205. Where possible, the roughed-out parts are finished with a fine shearing cut made with the skew chisel.

Fig. 206. The taper is roughed out with a gouge and finished with the skew.

Note the fine, long shavings—a good indication of proper tool use.

Fig. 207. Sand the part thoroughly.

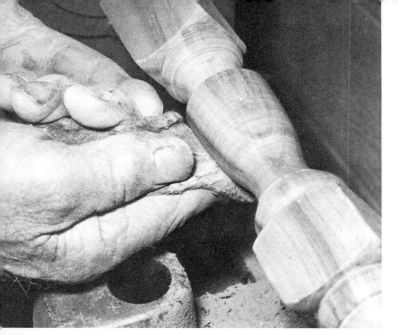

Fig. 208. Finish with steel wool.

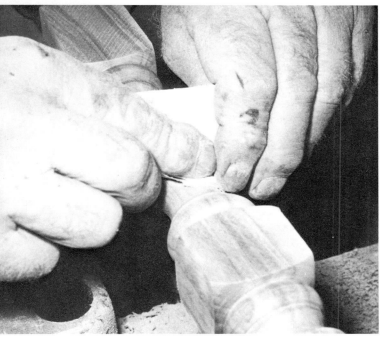

Fig. 209. Remove any remaining scratches by using a fine abrasive paper, sanding lightly *with* the grain.

Fig. 210. A fine example of a turning with rectangular sections.

Only the flat surfaces need to be sanded, and the leg is ready for use.

by E. N. Pearson

70

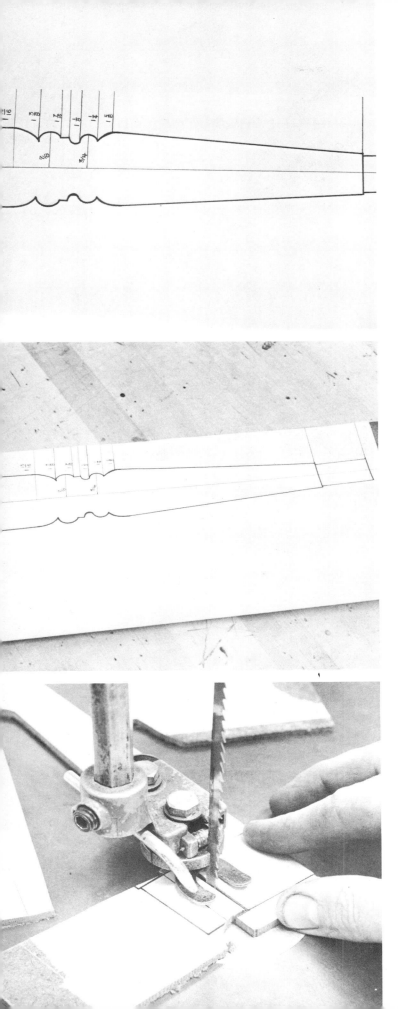

Duplicate Turnings

The woodturner often must make duplicate parts. These are commonly required for legs, posts, spindles, or articles such as candle holders or salad bowls. It will greatly increase accuracy and production speed if a template is constructed and used to lay out the dimensions and to check the profile of the turned piece. Templates may be full length, as used on a leg or spindle, or cross-sectional. Templates are always constructed full size, the template usually representing one-half of the turning.

Templates are commonly made from 1/8 inch tempered hardboard. This material is hard and durable, providing a template which can be used many times. The template should be laid out with extreme care and accuracy, since an error in the design or measurements of the template will be reproduced in the turning.

It is common practice to plan and lay out the pattern on a piece of heavy paper or light cardboard. This pattern is then glued to the masonite surface. The pattern should include all measurements necessary for completion of the turning.

Fig. 211. The first step in making a template is to make a full-size pattern of the turning. This must be drawn accurately, as the pattern becomes the template.

Use a piece of heavy paper and draw the full-size pattern parallel to the top edge of the paper and 1½ to 2 inches away from the edge.

Extend the profile break lines to the top edge of the paper. These lines are used to transfer dimensions to the stock.

Fig. 212. Joint one edge of a piece of 1/8 inch hardboard and glue the pattern to the hardboard.

The top edge of the pattern must be even with the jointed edge of the hardboard.

Fig. 213. Using a jig saw, cut the template to shape. Remember to cut on the inside of the pattern, leaving the line completely on the pattern. A small shoulder at each end of the template may be useful in laying out and checking the turning for dimension, shape, and fit.

Fig. 214. File and sand the template to final shape.

Be sure all curves are smooth and round.

It may be desirable to chamfer the underside edges of the template to allow for a more accurate fit to the turning.

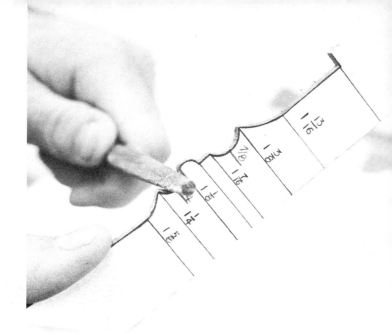

Fig. 215. Select a piece of stock suitable for making the turning. Turn the stock to rough diameter, allowing about 1/16 inch for smoothing and sanding.

Fig. 216. Move the tool rest to within 1/16 to 1/8 inch of the stock.

Position the template against the stock and start the lathe at slowest speed.

Hold the template firmly in position and, with a pencil, transfer the profile break lines to the stock.

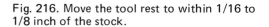

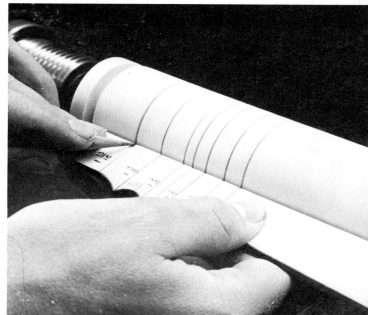

 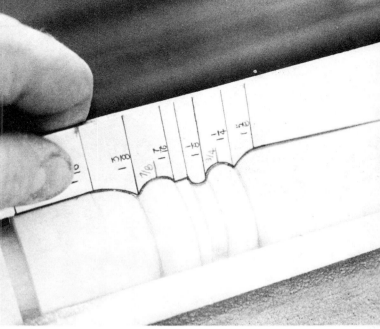

Fig. 217. With a parting tool and calipers, establish the high diameters for the beads or shoulders, and the low diameters of the coves. Allow 1/16 to 1/8 inch for clean-up cuts and sanding.

Fig. 218. Using the necessary tools, complete the turning. Check often with the template. Remember, it is easier to take a little wood off the turning than it is to put it back on.

by Dale L. Nish

Faceplate Turning: Centering and Mounting the Stock on a Metal Faceplate

A common method of holding stock for faceplate turning is to use screws to fasten the stock to a metal faceplate.

Faceplates come in several sizes, with different hole spacings to receive the screws. Select a faceplate slightly smaller than the base of the finished object, and locate the screws so they will not protrude through the finished base.

Fig. 219. Select a piece of stock, and square it up, allowing at least ¼ inch for trueing up the stock and laying out the circle.

Using a hand plane or jointer, true one side of the stock.

Fig. 220. Using a combination square or straightedge, mark diagonals to locate the center point.

Fig. 221. Lay out and mark the circle.

The diameter should be at least 1/8 to ¼ inch larger than the finished dimensions.

Fig. 222. Using a band saw, cut the stock to rough shape. Remember to cut in the waste stock.

Fig. 223. Select a faceplate of proper size, and measure its diameter.

Fig. 224. Set the compass 1/16 inch more than one half the diameter of the faceplate.

Mark a circle on the stock, using the center point established previously.

Fig. 225. Center the faceplate on the stock.

Rotate the faceplate until no two screws are in line with the grain of the wood.

Mark the holes.

Fig. 226. Using a nail set, or drill, make holes where the screw holes have been marked.

Stock less than 6 inches in diameter requires 2 or 3 screws.

Larger diameter stock requires more screws. The number required depends on faceplate size and the diameter and thickness of stock.

Fig. 227. Select a screw that has a diameter equal to the hole size in the faceplate.

Small screws in large holes may allow the stock to work loose and vibrate while turning.

The screw should be as long as possible, up to a maximum penetration of 1 inch of the screw actually in the wood.

Be sure the screws do not penetrate deep enough to be hit by a lathe tool.

Also, do not punch or bore the holes so deep as to show on the finished surface of the turning.

Fig. 228. Drive the screw in until it is in as far as it will go.

Protruding screw heads are dangerous and must be avoided.

Fastening Stock to a Faceplate, Glue Method

The most common way to fasten stock to a faceplate is with screws. At times, however, this method is undesirable for the following reasons:

1. The stock is too thin to be fastened directly to the faceplate.

2. Screw holes are objectionable.

3. Screws may hit the lathe tools.

4. The project requires the maximum thickness of stock.

5. The project necessitates cutting through the stock and into the faceplate, as in circular picture frames.

6. The project is of segmented construction, and must be glued to a wooden base.

The following procedure is commonly used, particularly when turning bowls or other projects which require the maximum thickness of the stock.

Fig. 229. Plane one side of the stock until it is flat.

Cut out a circular piece of waste stock (auxiliary faceplate), larger than the faceplate and smaller than the diameter of the workpiece.

Cut out a piece of light cardboard or heavy paper the same diameter as the auxiliary faceplate.

Fig. 230. Drive a finish nail through the center of the auxiliary faceplate.

The nail is used to center the faceplate with the workpiece.

Fig. 231. Place a light coat of glue on the auxiliary faceplate.

Fig. 232. Center the cardboard over the nail point and push the cardboard against the glued surface.

Place a light coat of glue on the cardboard.

Fig. 233. Place the glued side of the cardboard against the workpiece.

Place the tip of the nail in the center point of the workpiece.

Drive the nail in ¼ inch or less. This will hold the auxiliary piece in position while the clamps are applied.

Clamp the auxiliary faceplate to the workpiece and set aside until the glue has set.

Fig. 234. Pull the finish nail.

Fasten the metal faceplate to the auxiliary (wooden) faceplate.

CAUTION: The screws must be as long as possible, but they must not go through the auxiliary faceplate and into the workpiece.

Glue Chucking

Glue chucking is an excellent method for fastening a cylinder to a faceplate. The method provides a strong joint, which allows a minimum of vibration during the turning process. It has application for projects such as candle lamps, salt shakers, pepper shakers, different types of round containers, or goblets.

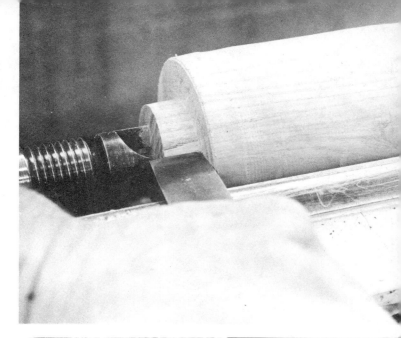

Fig. 235. Mount the stock between centers and turn the stock until it is cylindrical.

Turn a stub spindle or plug on one end of the cylinder. This end will become the bottom of the turning.

The plug is about 1¼ to 1½ inches in diameter and ½ to ¾ inches long.

Fig. 236. Select a scrap piece of solid stock, preferably hardwood. Lay out a circle a little larger than the diameter of the faceplate. The diameter will vary according to the stock to be turned.

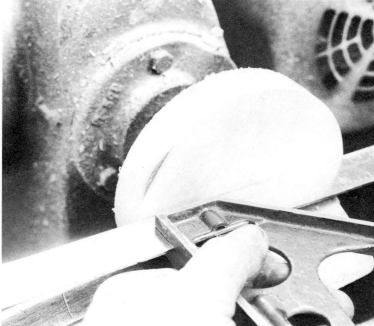

Cut the stock to rough size and mount securely to a faceplate. Select large screws which will penetrate the full thickness of the stock. Remember, glue chucking is to provide a solid method of fastening a cylinder to a faceplate. The turning is generally end grain, which is difficult. The screws must hold without splitting and pulling loose.

Turn the stock to a complete circle.

Face the stock flat and true.

Check with a straightedge tool.

Fig. 237. Bore a hole in the base piece. The hole must be exactly the size of the plug.

The hole may be bored with a bit if the correct size is available, or may be bored with a skew or squarenose chisel.

Be accurate. A loose fit is not adequate for this operation.

Place glue inside the hole in the base piece, as well as on the plug and shoulder of the work piece.

Fig. 238. Place the pieces together, then screw the faceplate onto the headstock.

Slide the tailstock into position and clamp securely.

Turn the cup center into the workpiece. Pressure from the cup center will act as a clamp and keep the stock centered while the glue dries.

The assembly should remain clamped on the lathe for at least one hour, then be set aside for 24 hours to allow the glue to set completely.

by Dale L. Nish

Ring Clamp Chuck

Fig. 239. The ring clamp chuck is an excellent method for holding cylindrical stock for heavy end-grain turning. The chuck is useful for turnings such as small containers, goblets, salt and pepper sets, egg cups, or small bowls. The chuck will hold the stock securely, with the advantage that the turning can be quickly removed if necessary, then replaced in the chuck and still be perfectly centered. The stock is supported around its circumference, thus giving maximum support at all times, yet the ring chuck clamp requires only hand tightening for most uses.

Fig. 240. Slip the chuck ring over the tailstock spindle, then place the rough stock between the lathe centers and turn to a rough cylinder.

Turn the right-hand end of the cylinder to a diameter equal to the flange opening of the chuck ring.

Fig. 241. Face the left-hand end of the cylinder smooth and true, with a flat or slightly concave surface.

Set the calipers to the diameter of the flange opening of the chuck ring. Good practice is to set the calipers directly from the right end of the cylinder, which was turned to size. It might be well to keep this setting slightly oversize to allow for final fitting.

Using a parting tool, cut a shoulder about ¼ inch in from the left end of the cylinder.

Check carefully with the calipers. Do not go under size.

Fig. 242. Working from the shoulder of the cylinder toward the right, remove the surplus stock until the chuck ring will slide along the cylinder.

The fit may be fairly loose along the cylinder, but the ring must be snug where the flange contacts the shoulder.

Fig. 243. Check for final fit.

Fig. 244. Facing off the left end may leave a little stock protruding in the area where the spur center was in contact with the end. Remove this stock with a sander or chisel.

Using the center hole left by the spur center, drill a small hole the diameter and length of the chuck center pin. This pin is used to keep the stock in perfect alignment if it needs to be removed, then replaced.

Fig. 245. Screw the threaded faceplate to the headstock spindle and center the stock on the faceplate.

Slip the clamp ring over the cylinder and screw the clamp ring to the faceplate.

Hand pressure is sufficient to hold the stock firmly and securely.

Fig. 246. This small container was turned quickly and efficiently with the use of the ring clamp chuck.

Further information on the actual turning is illustrated in the sequence "Small Round Boxes," page 140.

Fig. 247. The complete unit, disassembled. This type of clamp is not available commercially, but a machinist can quickly make one, using a faceplate from a wood lathe. The faceplate should have fine threads, as they hold better and can be tightened with less pressure. This chuck has 13 threads to the inch. More could be effectively used.

Faceplate Turning: Reducing to Outside Diameter

Fig. 248. Fasten the stock to the faceplate.

Mount the stock on the lathe and tighten the faceplate to the spindle.

Fig. 249. Set the tool rest just above the center of the spindle.

Turning the stock by hand, move the tool rest in until it clears all parts of the stock by 1/8 inch.

Move the tailstock into position. Lock, then turn the dead center into the stock. This will help steady the stock while turning. It may also help avoid an accident, particularly if the stock has been glued to an auxiliary faceplate.

Fig. 250. Start the machine and run at lowest speed.

Place the gouge on the tool rest, and take a light cut across the face of the stock.

Repeat the cuts until the stock begins to become cylindrical.

Fig. 251. Make a series of cuts on the right side of the stock.

Repeat the cuts until the stock is cylindrical at that point. This will indicate the maximum diameter of the cylinder.

Repeat the cuts across the edge of the stock; continue until the stock is cylindrical and at rough diameter.

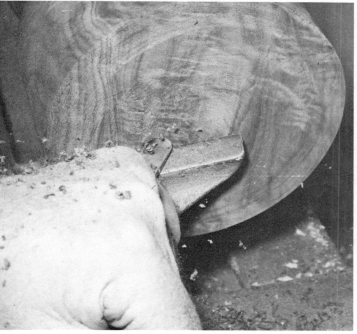

Fig. 252. Adjust the tool rest until it is parallel to the face of the stock.

Do not change the height of the tool rest.

Turn the stock by hand, checking to be sure the 1/8" clearance is maintained.

Using the roundnose chisel, make a series of cuts from the center of the face to the outer edge.

Fig. 253. Check the face with a straightedge.

For most faceplate turning this may not be necessary. However, it is always good practice to true the face at least part way in from the edge.

Boring

The lathe is commonly used for boring operations, since it can accomplish this work quickly, accurately, and easily. The lathe is in fact much like a drill press. Holes or recesses may be bored in various ways, such as with the skew chisel, the four-jaw chuck, and the geared or Jacobs chuck.

The skew is used by itself. The chucks require use of various types of drill bits, depending on the operation to be performed. In general, the bits used must not have a screw point, as such a point may force itself into the stock and cause it to split, or the hole left by the point itself may be undesirable.

Boring with the Skew

Fig. 254. The skew is often used to bore small holes in faceplate turning. It may also be used to bore large recesses such as in bowls or goblets. The procedure is basically the same.

Mark the center point of the stock.

Set the dividers or compass to the desired radius.

Using the center mark as a pivot point, mark the outline of the hole.

Fig. 255. Adjust the tool rest and hold the skew chisel in flat position, point against the stock.

Start cutting at the center of the stock, and work out to the outside edge.

Remove the stock in small amounts until the rough diameter of the opening has been reached.

Fig. 256. Finish the hole by holding the skew at 90° to the face of the stock.

Take light cuts with the point of the tool, using the side of the skew as a guide.

Fig. 257. Check the hole for correct diameter, using vernier calipers, inside calipers, or the piece which is to fit into the hole.

Fig. 258. **Boring with the Geared Chuck**
For boring into faceplate turnings, the geared chuck is placed in the tailstock of the lathe and firmly seated into the spindle.

Fig. 259. Select a drill bit with the desired diameter. A multispur bit is a good choice for this operation.

Fig. 260. Turn the tailstock handwheel, and bring the tailstock spindle back into the tailstock as far as possible without loosening the chuck.

Insert the bit into the chuck and tighten securely.

Move the tailstock assembly into position.

The bit should be approximately ¼ inch from the stock.

Tighten the tailstock clamp.

Start the lathe and feed the bit into the stock by turning the handwheel.

Fig. 261. Frequently take out the bit to remove the shavings.

Fig. 262. **Boring with the Geared Chuck and the Four-Jaw Chuck**
The four-jaw chuck is often used to hold the stock for boring.

For best results the stock should be turned to a cylindrical shape.

Fasten the stock in the chuck.

Clamp securely, tightening the chuck with the chuck key.

Fig. 263. For large holes being bored in end grain, it is best to bore a hole approximately 1/8" diameter less than the finished hole size.

Use either a Foerstner or multispur bit.

Bore the smaller hole using the same procedure as in boring a hole in a faceplate turning (see sequence "Boring with the Geared Chuck," page 89).
Change to the larger bit and bore the hole to finished size.

Sanding

The cleaner and smoother the turning of a piece, the less sanding is required. Stock shaped with a shearing cut requires little sanding while turnings made by scraping require more sanding before applying the finish. The grit size used in beginning sanding will depend on the condition of the turning.

It is good practice to sand with used sandpaper, as the grit is not so sharp, and is less likely to leave rings around the stock. If new sandpaper is used, rub the grit surfaces together before using. Rubbing will help dull any long abrasive particles, and deep scratches will be reduced.

The kind and size of abrasive selected will vary according to the kind of wood, the quality of the job, and the preference and experience of the operator.

Satisfactory sanding usually can be accomplished with the use of three grit sizes of sandpaper. The first or rough sanding is completed with #80 or #100 grit; the second, with #150 or #180 grit; the third and final sanding, with #220 or #280 grit. Final touching up is usually done *with* the grain, sanding lightly and using #220 or #280 grit.

Do not change to a finer grit until the grit you are using will no longer improve the surface of the turning. The most common mistake in sanding is to change to finer grits too quickly.

Fig. 264. Always move the tool rest out of the way before beginning to sand. This will allow you to work safely and easily, without getting your fingers caught between the stock and the tool rest.

Fig. 265. For most sanding tear a full sheet of abrasive paper into fourths.

Fold each fourth in thirds, crosswise, carefully matching the folded edges.

This is the basic shape for sanding.

Fig. 266. Large coves and beads may be sanded by shaping the folded sandpaper into a U shape.

The radius on the fold should be slightly smaller than the cove or bead.

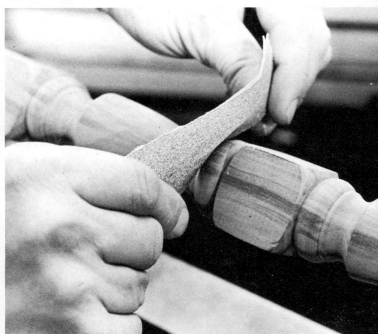

Fig. 267. Holding the paper between the thumb and forefinger, sand the cove or bead.

Be careful not to sand parts other than that intended.

Fig. 268. Small coves or beads can be sanded by wrapping a piece of sandpaper around a dowel.

Fig. 269. Beads or round shoulders are sanded with abrasive paper held in vertical position.

Fig. 270. Then roll paper to the left or right, shaping and sanding the bead.

92

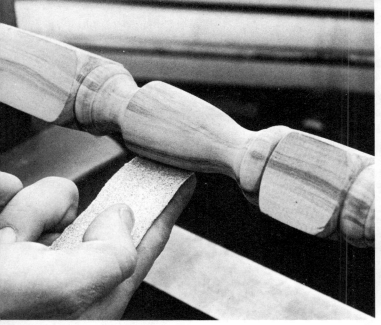

Fig. 271. Flat areas or shoulders are sanded with the paper in flat position.

Be careful not to sand adjacent parts of the turning.

Fig. 272. Flat surfaces, such as tapers, can be quickly sanded.

These surfaces usually require a light sanding with fine paper and a stopped lathe.

Fig. 273. Circular scratches may be quite prominent on large surfaces and must be removed by sanding with the grain.

CAUTION: It is extremely easy during sanding to remove the crisp, sharp lines of the turning. Try to keep all the lines sharp and clearly defined. An expert sanding job will leave the surfaces smooth, but each with its own shape and line.

Fig. 274. You may find a small pad of steel wool placed between the sandpaper and the fingers will help keep the fingers from getting hot as a result of friction from the sanding process.

This is particularly useful while sanding flat surfaces.

Fig. 275. Sanding bowls requires the same sequence of abrasive grits as other sanding jobs; begin with #80, then go on to #100, #150 and #220.

For larger bowls it is best to use a quarter of a sheet of abrasive paper folded in half, with a pad of steel wool to reduce the heat transmitted to the fingers.

Use uniform pressure, moving back and forth across the surface of the bowl.

As the paper becomes loaded or worn, select a new surface for contact with the bowl.

Fig. 276. The inside of the bowl is sanded in a manner similar to that used on the outside.

It is advisable to fold the paper in thirds, owing to the restricted area inside the bowl. Use a steel wool pad to protect the fingers from heat.

Fig. 277. When you are satisfied with the final surface of the bowl, stop the lathe and sand with the grain of the wood.

Use a coarser grit than that employed for the finish sanding. For example, if the last paper used was #220, use #180 or #150 for sanding with the grain.

Fig. 278. The outside of the bowl should also be sanded with the grain to remove circular scratches. These are most noticeable on the end grain.

Removing stubborn scratches is easily accomplished with the use of a sanding block. *Caution:* Do not sand flat spots into the surface of the bowl.

Finishing Wood Turnings

The finish of a wood turning job can be no better than the surface provided by the final sanding operation. In fact, the finishing process will accent defects such as torn grain, irregular surfaces, or sanding scratches. A quality sanding job is essential for a fine finish.

Most finishing processes can be used on lathe work. However, avoid processes which alter the original color of the wood. Stains and bleaches should not be used unless their use is essential to match other stained or bleached pieces. The natural color and grain pattern of wood are its best qualities. Don't alter them. Surface finishes such as varnish, lacquer, polyurethane, or shellac may be used. A favorite finish of mine is Fullerplast, satin or semi-gloss. Whichever finish you choose, it should be water-clear, without the tendency to yellow or discolor with age. It should also be resistant to water and common household wood polishes or cleaners, and should be scratch resistant.

Penetrating wood finishes such as Watco Danish Oil work well on turnings. They are useful where a quick finish is desired, or where a high gloss finish is not required. Oil finishes tend to darken the wood, in some cases obscuring the natural wood grain. In other woods, the grain pattern is accented by the oil. Naturally oily woods, such as teak, benefit by an oil finish. Dark woods, such as walnut, often lose contrast and grain pattern when oiled. Experiment on a scrap before finishing the project.

Another factor to keep in mind is that penetrating oil finishes actually harden in the wood and become part of it. Periodic applications of oil improve the appearance each time the oil is applied and the piece polished. Over the years, oiled pieces have a patina and richness not achieved in surface finishes. The oiled surfaces improve with age, whereas surface finishes tend to deteriorate.

Kitchenware or other turnings used in contact with foods must have non-toxic finishes. One of the best is cooking or salad oil. Avoid natural oils, such as olive oil. These may become rancid with age and cause a piece to be ruined because of rancid odor and taste.

Wax is used where a cheap, quick finish is desired. This is not a durable finish, and is not recommended for most turnings.

French polish, which is a mixture of shellac and linseed oil, may be used on turnings; however, this finish is difficult to work with.

For further information on finishes consult a good wood-finishing book.

FINISHING A BOWL (surface finish)

Fig. 279. Sand the bowl to final finish, generally up to #180 or #220 grit abrasive paper.

Final sanding should be with the grain of the wood.

Fig. 280. Open grain woods may require a paste filler. If so, apply the filler liberally to the bowl, working it into the pores of the wood.

Fig. 281. Allow the filler to lose its shiny, wet gloss, then pad the filler into the pores.

Remove excess filler from the surface of the bowl with a coarse cloth.

Fig. 282. Carefully fold a pad as shown, leaving no loose corners or edges.

Start the lathe and remove the remaining filler from the bowl. The speed of the bowl turning will leave a semi-polished surface.

Be sure all streaks and filler are removed.

Set the bowl aside to dry for 24 hours.

Fig. 283. Spray the underside of the bowl with a wet, uniform coat of finish. Avoid sags or runs.

Notice the bowl is still on the faceplate. It is not removed from the faceplate until the finishing is complete.

Fig. 284. Place the bowl on a spray table and spray the inside with a wet, uniform coat, avoiding sags and runs.

Let the bowl dry, then re-coat.

Set aside to dry for at least 24 hours. The finish must be hard before sanding.

Even if all rough spots cannot be removed during the first sanding, use caution.

DO NOT SAND THROUGH THE FINISH!

Fig. 285. Place the bowl on the lathe and sand lightly with #220 grit open coat paper. Be particularly careful on the edges of the turning, as a sand-through may necessitate complete resanding, removing the finish, and repeating the finishing operation.

Fig. 286. Wipe or blow most of the sanding dust from the bowl.

Using a tack rag, carefully remove the remaining traces of dust.

Repeat the spraying process.

Four to six coats should provide an excellent finish.

Fig. 287. Place the bowl on the lathe, and sand with #400 grit wet or dry silicone carbide paper. This sanding should leave the bowl perfectly smooth. Use water liberally as a lubricant.

Repeat sanding, with #600 grit wet or dry silicone carbide paper. Use plenty of water.

Dry the surface with a clean cloth, and carefully examine it for defects. If you are satisfied with the surface, proceed with finishing; if not, more sanding may be necessary. In extreme cases, another coat of finish may need to be applied, and the above steps repeated.

Fig. 288. The final finish is a coat of high quality paste wax. The wax is applied with a pad of 0000 steel wool, with the lathe running. The steel wool will cut down the gloss of the surface. If a high gloss is desired, apply the wax with a soft cotton pad.

Allow the wax to dry for 10 to 15 minutes, start the lathe and polish the turning with a soft, dry cloth.

Fig. 289. If an oil finish is desired, saturate a pad with oil and apply liberally to the surface of the wood. When dull spots appear, apply more oil. Continue the application for 15 to 20 minutes, or until it seems the wood will not absorb more oil.

Select a clean, dry cloth and wipe the excess oil from the wood.

Start the lathe and polish the turning. The friction from the rotating wood will cause the wood to polish to a smooth satin finish.

Fig. 290. A preferred method of applying oil, if the project is small or sufficient oil is available, is to immerse the turning in an oil bath for a period of time, possibly overnight. The oil will penetrate deep into the wood. The project is then removed from the oil, drained and wiped clean.

Replace the turning onto the lathe and polish until it is dry and smooth.

Fig. 291. A quick, efficient and inexpensive method of finishing some turnings is to apply paste wax directly to the wood. Apply the wax liberally, and allow to dry for a few minutes. Start the lathe and polish with a pad. The pressure from the pad should cause the wax to melt and penetrate the wood. Further polishing will give a soft, smooth finish. Repeat the process if necessary.

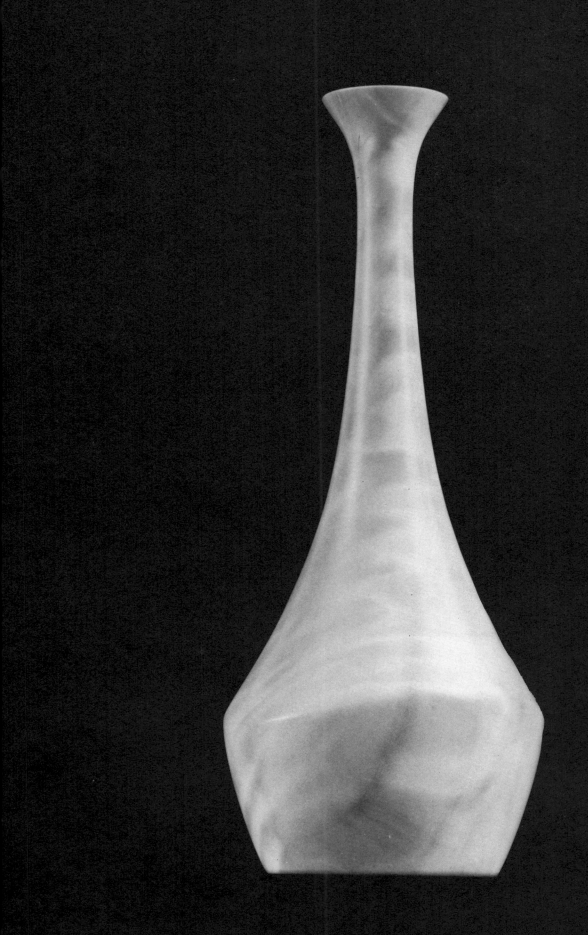

by Dale L. Nish

Oval Turnings

Fig. 292. Oval turning can be used for handles, furniture legs, or decor items such as bud vases. The principle is the same, while the end use may be different.

Fig. 293. The stock selected must be an accurately cut rectangle. The four surfaces are bisected as shown, with the lines extending the length of the stock. The lines extending end to end are called ridge lines.

The true center is the point where the lines intersect.

The compass is then set and positioned near the true center, but on the short axis of the bisecting lines.

Experiment with different compass settings and positions on the short axis. When you are satisfied, mark two points equidistant from the center and draw the arcs.

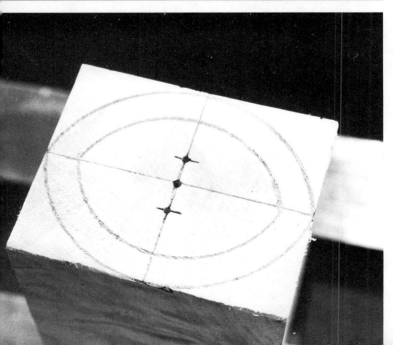

Fig. 294. For a simple oval, one set of arcs is sufficient. For a project with size variation, use the same centers but draw another set of arcs.

This may be repeated on the other end of the block, if a full length oval is required.

In some projects, one end only is marked, with the other end turning at the true center.

Fig. 295. Place the turning between the lathe centers, with the dead center positioned as shown.

Fig. 296. Move the tool rest into position, allowing sufficient clearance for the turning to rotate.

Rotate the turning by hand, being certain that no part of the stock touches the tool rest.

Start the lathe and remove the wood to a point touching the ridge line. Frequent checking is advisable, as it is easy to remove too much stock.

Fig. 297. Change centers and remove the other side of the stock.

The ridge line should be left to indicate the center of the oval.

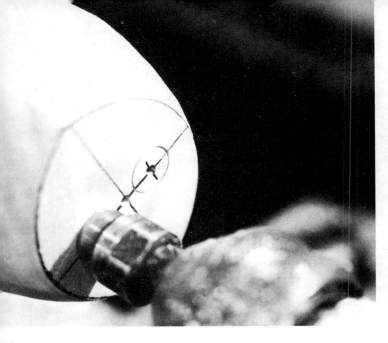

Fig. 298. If necessary, establish the point for the second oval to start and repeat the turning sequence, changing centers when necessary.

The bud vase being turned here may require different diameter ovals.

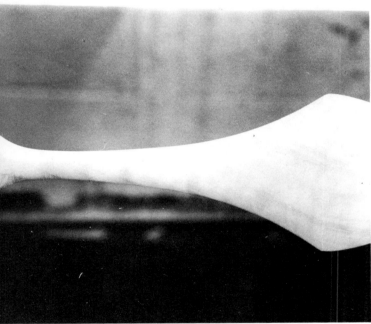

Fig. 299. When the ovals have been turned, replace the turning at the true center and complete the operation.

Sand completely. A thorough sanding job will blend the ovals into the round areas, as well as blend out the ridge lines.

A slow sanding speed is best.

by Dale L. Nish

Split Turnings

The split-turning technique is used where two identical semicircular pieces are required. One method is to make a complete turning from solid stock, and saw the turning into halves, but the saw kerf and smoothing operation will reduce the size of each piece.

A preferred method is to join two pieces of stock with glue, with paper placed between the two pieces. The paper and glue will hold the pieces together, with the paper allowing the two pieces to be easily split apart when the turning is completed. If four identical quarters are required, use the same method for joining four pieces together. Special care should be taken to insure that the joints intersect the center of the stock.

Fig. 300. Select stock suitable for each half of the split turning. Cut the pieces to identical size and prepare for gluing.

Cut out a piece of light cardboard or magazine cover a little larger than the pieces.

Fig. 301. Apply an even coat of glue to one surface.

Place the cardboard on the glued surface.

Spread an even coat of glue on the cardboard.

Place the second piece of stock on the card-board, carefully align the pieces, and clamp securely.

Set aside to dry for at least 24 hours. The heavy glue and paper line must be completely dry before turning the piece.

Fig. 302. Draw diagonal lines on each end of the stock.

These lines must bisect at the paper and glue line. If not, adjust the lines until they do.

Drill a pilot hole where the lines intersect. This hole will help prevent the center from splitting the turning.

Place the spur center in position with the prongs following the diagonal lines. This position allows the prongs to help hold the turning together. If the prongs enter the paper and glue line, the stock will probably split.

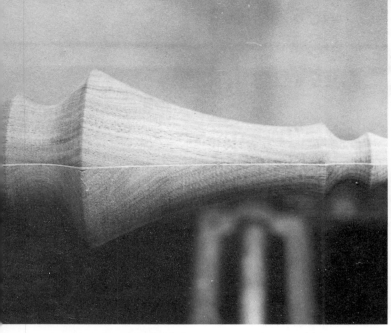

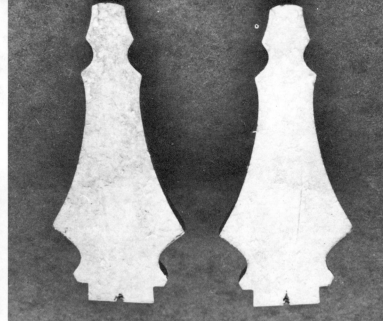

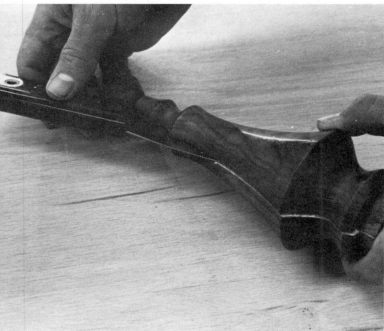

Fig. 303. Turn at low speed being careful not to catch a tool in the stock.

Complete the turning using normal turning methods.

Sand the turning completely, and, if desired, the turning may be finished.

Fig. 304. Split the turning, using a thin knife. Use caution, particularly if there are thin or weak areas in the turning. Light, steady pressure will do the job.

Fig. 305. The identical parts will have a thin layer of paper on the back of each piece. This may be removed by sanding, or may be left on the stock.

Fig. 306. Two circular halves such as the tops for wall shelves may be turned together and then split.

Cut a strip of paper of suitable size to separate the two pieces.

Apply glue to each edge of the stock, insert the paper and clamp the assembly securely.

Set aside until completely dry. This will take at least 24 hours.

Fig. 307. Lay out and cut the stock to the required diameter, allowing for truing up the circle.

Cut out a piece of waste stock the size of the faceplate.

Cut out a piece of paper the size of the faceplate.

Lay out a circle a little smaller than the hole to be bored for joining the base to the top.

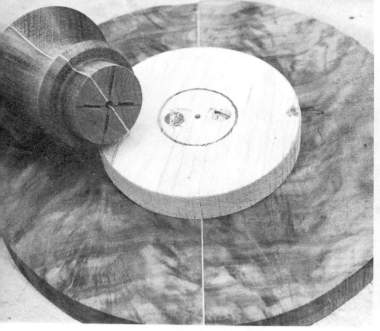

Drill pilot and shank holes for 2 screws used to fasten the waste stock to the turning. Keep the screw holes well inside the circle.

Glue the waste stock to the turning with the paper disc between the two pieces.

Install the screws. They will hold the waste stock in position until the glue dries. They will also act as insurance against splitting during the turning of the stock.

Fig. 308. Fasten the faceplate to the waste piece. The screws should not penetrate the turning stock.

Set the assembly aside to allow the glue to dry completely.

Fig. 309. Use a slow turning speed, with particular caution not to force the turning or catch a tool in the stock.

While turning, do not stand in line with the rotating stock. The procedure is safe, but precautions should be observed. If any evidence of vibration or delamination occurs, stop the lathe immediately and examine the stock carefully.

When the turning is complete, sand and apply the desired finish.

Bore the required hole for assembly with the base piece.

Use a thin knife and split the turning.

Fig. 310. Glue the base piece into the top piece.

The fit should be exact.

by Dale L. Nish

Working with Unseasoned Wood

Unseasoned (green) wood is available everywhere, and compared with the seasoned variety, at greatly reduced cost to the turner. Wood from fruit trees such as cherry, apple, apricot, and peach is available in fruit-growing areas. Wood from shade trees, such as elm, ash, sycamore, locust, walnut, poplar, catalpa, and maple is available from tree-removal companies, local saw mills, private land owners, and others. Each part of the country has native hardwoods capable of producing excellent turning stock. In fact, local sources of green wood have potential for wood with high figure and color that probably is not available from other sources. Stumps, burls, and even tree limbs also may be sources of beautiful turning stock. The resourceful wood turner will be constantly on the lookout for new sources of wood.

When a supplier of unseasoned wood is found, show appreciation by giving him a finished turning or two, and you will be repaid many times with a new friend and a continuing supply of material.

Some woodturners always select wood that is free from pith, knots, or sapwood. Such wood is easiest to turn, but may lack some of the beauty of wood with knots or sapwood. Sapwood may add interest and contrast to a rather plain piece. Keep in mind, however, that sapwood and knots increase the difficulty in seasoning green wood.

If a wood is free from defects—that is, without knots or sapwood to interfere with the desired shape—it is best to turn out the inside of the bowl following the curve of the annual rings. The curve is determined by looking at the end grain of the stock. A rough-turned bowl will tend to curve inward when drying, and annual rings tend to straighten when drying. Thus, a bowl turned following the curve of the annual rings will tend to distort less during drying than one turned against the curve of the annual rings. However, if defects or other circumstances develop so that the bowl cannot be turned with the annual rings, turn the bowl against the curve of the rings. There will be more distortion during drying, but the bowl will probably stay within the tolerance necessary to complete the turning.

Green wood, fresh from the tree, can be roughed out, dried, and finished in approximately three months. One method of accomplishing this is with the use of paste wax. The wax will partially seal the surface of the rough turning, particularly end grain, where most checking occurs. This partial sealing allows the rough turning to dry out slowly and uniformly, reducing or eliminating checking.

Fig. 311. These bowls were turned green, dried, and ready for finishing in less than three months. They are free from defects, and the only procedure used was to turn them green then liberally coat the surface with paste wax.

Fig. 312. This bowl was turned green, and allowed to dry under the same conditions as the bowls above except that it was not coated with paste wax. Note the extreme shrinkage and checking.

Fig. 313. This bowl was turned from partially dry catalpa wood. The surface was coated with paste wax, the bowl placed on a shelf and allowed to dry. To check the rate of drying, the bowl was weighed periodically.

10-31 1743 grams (partially dry weight)
11-7   1460 grams (loss of 283 grams water in 7 days)
11-27 1360 grams (loss of 100 grams water in 20 days)
1-26   1350 grams (loss of 10 grams water in 61 days)

The bowl was completed on 2-1, when weighing indicated no further weight loss.

Fig. 314. This bowl was turned from green Chinese Elm wood. The surface was coated with paste wax, the bowl placed on a shelf in the shop and allowed to dry. Periodic weighing indicated weights as follows:

10-31 1800 grams (green weight)
11-7   1380 grams (loss of 420 grams water in 7 days)
11-26 1020 grams (loss of 360 grams water in 19 days)
1-26   980 grams (loss of 40 grams water in 60 days)

Fig. 315. This bowl was turned from green walnut limb wood, the surface coated with paste wax, the bowl placed on a shelf and allowed to dry. Periodic weighing indicated weights as follows:

12-3   570 grams (green weight)
12-24 410 grams (loss of 160 grams water in 21 days)
1-26   370 grams (loss of 40 grams water in 32 days)
2-8   365 grams (loss of 5 grams water in 13 days)

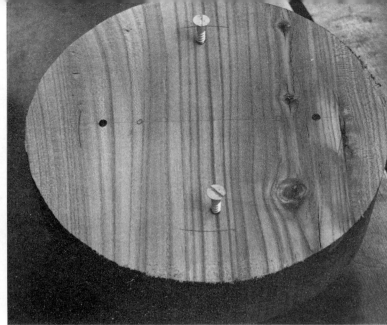

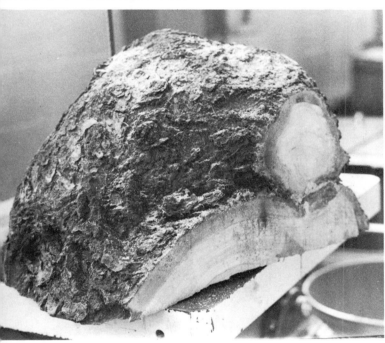

Fig. 316. During the drying process, the bowl will become elliptical in shape. On a bowl 12 inches in diameter, the difference in diameter across the grain and with the grain will be about 3/8'' to 1/2 inch. Leaving the wall thickness on a 12-inch bowl at 1 to 1¼ inches should allow sufficient material for trueing the turning and completing the project. In general, small bowls will shrink less and larger ones more. Different woods will shrink more, or less, depending on the species and growing conditions.

Fig. 317. Select a piece of green wood, such as this cherry burl, and band saw the stock to rough shape.

Fig. 318. Fasten the stock to the faceplate with screws, positioning two of the screws in line with the grain of the wood. During the drying process these two holes will remain in alignment and may be used to fasten the cured stock to the faceplate for the finish turning. Holes not in line with the grain will move considerably during the drying process, and probably will not line up with the holes in the faceplate.

Fig. 319. The wood selected should not contain the pith of the tree, as checking will radiate from the pith, and probably ruin the stock during drying.

Fig. 320. Turn the outside of the stock to the desired shape. Complete the inside of the turning, leaving a fairly uniform wall thickness of about 1 inch. Avoid extra thick or thin sections, as they will not dry uniformly with the rest of the rough turning, and may cause checking which would not otherwise occur.

Fig. 321. When the turning has been roughed out, take a handful of paste wax and liberally coat the turning, inside and outside. Remove the turning from the faceplate, and wax the bottom.

Fig. 322. Place the turning on a shelf, away from heat or air movement. Examine carefully for the first few days. If evidence of checking appears, apply more paste wax. Wood with extreme figures such as burls or stump wood may have to be waxed several times. With plain wood, or wood that has partially dried before turning, one coat is usually sufficient.

Another method of stabilizing green wood, thereby reducing the dimensional changes which occur during the drying process, is called PEG. This process was developed at the Forest Products Laboratory at Madison, Wisconsin, and was named after the primary material, polyethylene glycol 1000—PEG. The chemical is purchased as a solid, white, waxlike substance which can be easily dissolved in warm water.

The PEG process consists of dissolving the polyethylene glycol in warm water, and obtaining either a 30% or 50% solution, by weight.

The wood is treated by soaking the green turned stock for a period of time in a vat containing a PEG solution during which the PEG replaces the water in the cells of the wood. At the conclusion of the soaking period, the turnings are removed and allowed to dry in a heated room. Usual drying time is from four to eight weeks depending on conditions and thickness of the stock.

Fig. 323. These bowls were turned when green, soaked in PEG, dried and finished in three to four months.

Fig. 324. Select a container suitable for a vat. Materials such as plastic, glass, ceramic, fiberglass, or wood should be used. Metals other than certain types of stainless steel should be avoided because the metal will react with the PEG, causing the solution to darken and stain the wood.

Since heating the solution will give best results, an electric heating element should be built into the vat.

A lid will help conserve heat and control evaporation.

Fig. 325. Dissolve the PEG in warm water and obtain either a 30 or 50 percent solution, by weight. The 30 percent solution will have a specific gravity of 1.05 at 60° F.; the 50 percent solution will have a specific gravity of 1.093 at 60° F.

Fig. 326. The soaking period depends on the temperature of the solution, PEG concentration, and the species and thickness of the wood. Lower density woods such as softwoods and the "soft" hardwoods require about ½ the soaking time of walnut, while the higher density hardwoods such as beech, maple, birch, and fruitwoods require a soaking period several times that of walnut. Very dense woods require increased temperatures and long soaking times for effective treatment. Some woods, such as cherry, will honeycomb at temperatures over 110°. Use caution when working with high temperatures. Experiment, and determine soaking times which meet your own requirements.

Solution concentration and temperature	Suggested period of soak for:	
	Walnut disks up to 9 inches in diameter and 1 to 1½ inches thick	Walnut disks over 9 inches in diameter and 2 to 3 inches thick
30 percent, 70° F.	20 days	60 days
50 percent, 70° F.	15 days	45 days
30 percent, 140° F.	7 days	30 days
50 percent, 140° F.	3 days	14 days

Fig. 327. Rough turn the project to a wall thickness from ¾ to 1 inch. Uniform wall thickness is desired, as extreme variation may cause problems resulting from uneven PEG penetration, as well as drying. Large solid sections such as candle holders require longer soaking for best results.

Fig. 328. At the end of the soaking period, remove the projects from the vat and allow them to drain. Place them on a screened shelf in a well-heated and well-ventilated room. Air drying time will vary according to the air temperature, humidity, and the thickness of the wall sections. One way to check if the turnings are dry is to weigh them periodically. When a stable weight is reached, they are dry enough to finish.

Fig. 329. Plane the base of the turning flat. Mount on a faceplate and complete the turning.

Fig. 330. PEG-treated wood should be finished with a polyurethane finish, since most other finishes are not compatible with the treated wood. Sand, finish, and polish in the usual manner.

by Dale L. Nish

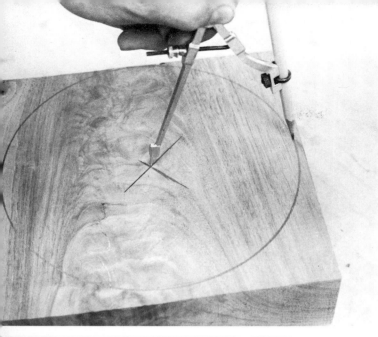

Turning a Deep Bowl

Fig. 331. Select a sound, seasoned block of wood of suitable dimensions for the bowl.

Mark the center of the stock.

Use a compass or dividers and mark out the circumference of the bowl.

Fig. 332. Bandsaw the bowl to rough shape.

If desired, the bandsaw table can be tilted to remove the excess stock from the bowl blank.

Fig. 333. Set the stops on the drill press so the drill bit will stop at the desired distance from the bottom of the bowl, normally about 1 inch.

Bore the hole.

This hole will constantly show the turner the required depth of the bowl, thus speeding up the turning process as measuring for depth is unnecessary. Also, the true center of the bowl is removed, allowing the tool to work into an open area. This makes turning the inside easier and faster.

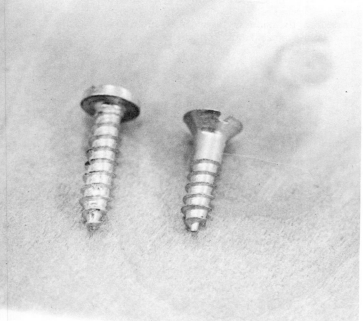

Fig. 334. Center the faceplate on the base of the bowl blank and mark the holes.

Fig. 335. Select the largest diameter screw which will go through the faceplate holes.

Sheet metal screws or flathead screws work well.

Screws with large, heavy threads will hold better than small screws. Shorter lengths can be used.

Fig. 336. Select a drill the size of the solid part of the screw inside the threads.

The screws should penetrate the wood from 1/2 to 5/8 inch. For most purposes this is adequate.

Drill the pilot holes *only* to the depth the screw will penetrate. Deep pilot holes may show up as holes in the bottom of the bowl.

Fig. 337. Fasten the faceplate securely to the bowl base.

Fig. 338. Mount the faceplate on the lathe and position the tool rest just above center.

Turn the bowl by hand to be sure the bowl is completely clear of the tool rest.

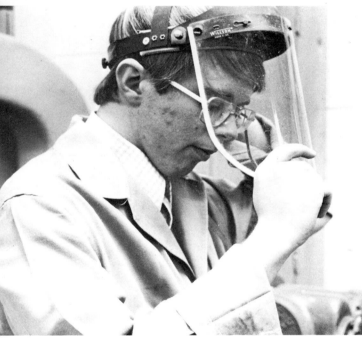

Fig. 339. Dress safely—sleeves rolled up, rings, ties, and watches removed, and face shield in place.

Fig. 340. Turn the bowl to a true circle, but do not remove more wood than is necessary.

Begin to shape the outside of the bowl.

Fig. 341. Keep the tool rest close to the bowl. This requires adjustment several times during the turning of the outside of the bowl.

Fig. 342. The final shaping cuts should be with a very sharp tool, taking very light cuts.

Fig. 343. Position the tool rest across the top of the bowl and about ¼ inch below center.

Fig. 344. Starting at the center of the bowl, make a series of cuts 1 to 1½ inches deep, progressing to the outside of the bowl.

Leave enough thickness of stock to meet the design requirements. The bowl shown in this sequence will have a wide, tapered rim, so the stock left may seem quite thick.

Fig. 345. When the outside has been reached, return to the center and make another series of cuts.

Fig. 346. As work progresses, adjust the tool rest so it goes into the bowl and better supports the tool.

The length of the tool protruding over the tool rest should be kept to a minimum to safeguard the turner *and* the tool.

Fig. 347. Select a sharp squarenose chisel and scrape the bottom of the bowl sure and flat.

Fig. 348. Adjust the tool rest to within ¼ inch of the side of the bowl.

Fig. 349. Use a roundnose chisel and shape the interior of the bowl to its final outline.

Fig. 350. Check the sides for uniform thickness. The top of the bowl is thin, gradually becoming thicker near the bottom.

The thickness of the parts of the bowl is largely determined by individual preference. Good design should be kept in mind, avoiding extremes in thickness or thinness.

Fig. 351. Sand the exterior of the bowl. Progress from coarse abrasive paper to medium to fine as sanding progresses. A good choice is #60 to 80 to 100 to 150 to 220 grit.

Do not move to a finer grit until the grit you are presently using will no longer improve the surface of the turning.

Remember—the most common mistake in sanding is to move to the finer grits too quickly.

Fig. 352. Sand the interior of the bowl, using the same procedure as outlined above.

It is possible to sand the inside and outside of the bowl at the same time, using a sanding pad in each hand.

When you are satisfied with the surfaces of the bowl, small circular scratches may be removed by sanding *with* the grain of the wood. This is desirable particularly on work of high quality.

At this point, the bowl is ready for finishing. See sequence "Finishing Wood Turnings," page 95.

by Dale L. Nish

124

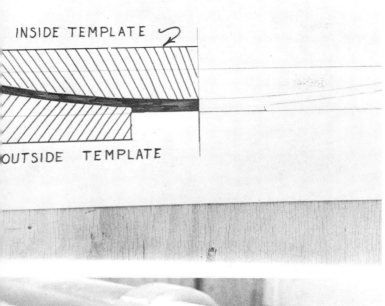

Turning a Shallow Bowl

Fig. 353. In turning a shallow bowl it is sometimes necessary to draw a sectional view of the bowl and convert the sectional drawing into a template.

This is necessary if several similar bowls are to be turned or the turner is not sure of the desired shape.

Fig. 354. Lay out the size of the bowl on stock of required dimensions.

Cut to size on the band saw.

Fasten the stock to the faceplate using the glue method or short screws.

Move the tailstock into position, using the dead center as a support during the turning operation.

Fig. 355. Adjust the tool rest to a position just above center of the stock.

Turn the stock to the required diameter, using a modified squarenose chisel, or diamond point.

Do not turn so much that the bowl becomes undersize!

Start to shape the outside of the bowl.

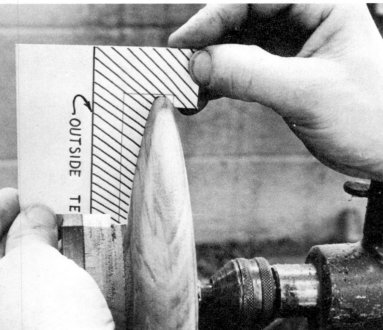

Fig. 356. Adjust the tool rest as shown, keeping it approximately ¼ to 3/8″ from the bowl.

Shape the outside of the bowl. A roundnose chisel works well for this operation.

Fig. 357. Check the outside shape frequently.

Allow enough stock for the sanding operation.

The outside of the bowl may be sanded now or later.

Fig. 358. Position the tool rest across the top of the bowl, with the tool rest just below the center.

Make the first cut about 1 to 1¼ inches in from the edge of the bowl, gradually moving the roundnose chisel to the rim of the bowl.

Repeat the above step until that portion of the bowl reaches final shape.

The purpose of this procedure is to leave the heavy stock in the center of the bowl, gradually working toward the center from the outside. This eliminates problems such as vibration and chatter, commonly associated with thin shallow sections.

Fig. 359. Check your progress with a template, or other method of testing for wall thickness.

Continue turning toward the center of the bowl.

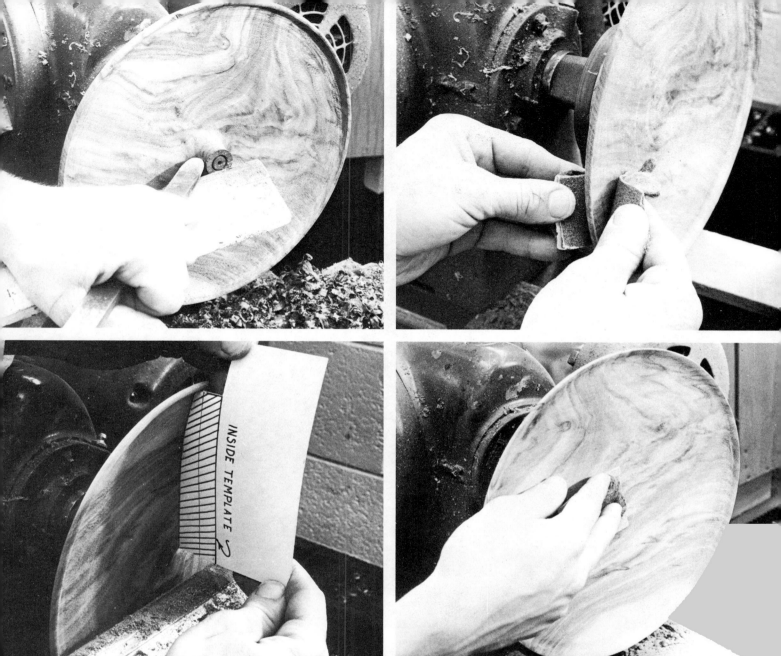

Fig. 360. Move the tailstock away from the bowl and remove the center portion.

Fig. 361. Make final check for shape.

Fig. 362. Thin, shallow bowls should be supported on both sides while sanding. Use a sanding pad on both sides.

Fig. 363. Final sanding should be with the grain of the wood, using light pressure. It is acceptable practice to use a more coarse grit while sanding with the grain. For example, if the final sanding was with # 220, then use # 180 for sanding with the grain. This will speed up the sanding operation and because you are sanding with the grain, the grit change will not be noticeable.

by Dale L. Nish

Rectangular Trays

Fig. 364. Rectangular or square trays can be turned on the lathe with little waste of material. The trays can be shaped after the turning is complete. These are generally large turnings, and are usually turned on the outboard end of the lathe.

Fig. 365. Select a piece of stock the required width and length of the tray.

Joint both edges, and glue waste stock on each edge to build the piece up to a square. The waste stock is for safety during turning, as the turning must be circular, or the tools may chip the edges, or grab and possibly cause an accident.

Lay out the circle, and cut to shape on the band saw.

Fig. 366. Fasten the stock to an outboard faceplate. In most cases, this will be the hand-wheel on the lathe.

Use short screws.

Turn the outside to desired shape, working from the outside edge, completing the shape as you work toward the center. This is the same procedure as used in turning shallow bowls.

Fig. 367. Turn the inside of the tray, working from the outside edge to the center. The turning must be complete as you work toward the center. Large shallow turnings such as this present considerable problems with chatter and vibration, if correct procedure is not used.

Fig. 368. Sand the tray, using a sanding block to give a flat smooth surface. Do not exert too much pressure, particularly toward the edges, as the tray is large and relatively thin.

Fig. 369. Remove the tray from the faceplate. At this point, the tray looks good enough to leave in its round shape.

Fig. 370. Remove the waste stock on the band saw.

If the tray has flat sides, plane them smooth, then sand completely, slightly rounding the sharp edges and blending the sides of the tray into the other surfaces.

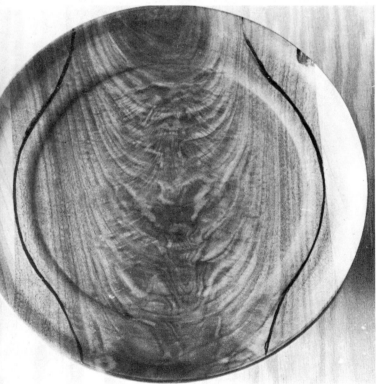

Fig. 371. The above procedure may be used for trays of various shapes. These shapes may develop from the grain pattern in the stock, or the intended use of the tray.

by Dale L. Nish

Shaping After Turning

Fig. 372. The bowls and the tray shown here were edge-shaped after the turning was complete. This technique will add interest and character to symmetrical turnings, if good design and craftsmanship are employed.

Fig. 373. The band saw is a useful tool in removing excess stock. If one is not available, a coping saw can be used.

Fig. 374. Sanders, such as the one pictured here, may be employed to smooth and shape the final contours. If not too much stock is to be removed, the sander may be used for the complete shaping process. Other types of sanders such as drum, disc, or spindle may be used effectively. If these are not available, hand tools such as rasps and files may do the job, with final sanding done by hand.

Hand sanding is necessary to blend the edges into the turned surfaces. All edges should be rounded and smooth. A hand feeling the surface of the turning should not encounter sharp, abrupt edges or surfaces. The project should be smooth, with each surface making a flowing transition to the next.

Lids

Fig. 375. An added touch of elegance to a rather plain container may be obtained by turning a lid. Lids can be turned in many shapes and sizes, but should be designed to be functional, as well as compatible with the lines of the container. Selecting highly figured wood for the lid may attract attention, or add emphasis to the appearance of the lid. Rather plain wood may be needed where the impact of the container is its shape. Choose the wood and design carefully.

There are many ways to turn lids. However, a lid should be lightweight, as well as beautiful. This sequence will illustrate how to turn a lid with a separate knob.

Fig. 376. Check the diameter of the opening to receive the lid, and cut out a rough circle using the band saw. The rough lid should be ¼ to ½ over the finished size.

Bore a pilot hole in the center of the lid and mount the lid on a screw center faceplate.

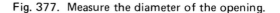

Fig. 377. Measure the diameter of the opening.

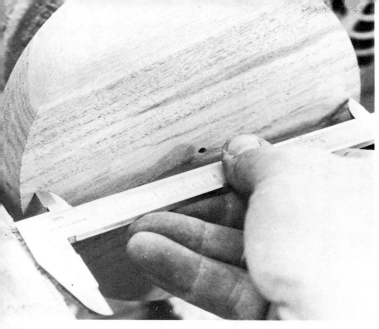

Fig. 378. Turn the disc to a true circle.

If necessary, face the disc until it is smooth and flat.

Transfer the diameter of the bowl opening to the lid.

Fig. 379. Turn the flange on the lid, being careful to keep the flange slightly larger in diameter than the bowl opening.

Use the bowl to check the flange for fit.

Using a sharp tool such as a squarenose, reduce the flange to the required size. At this point, the lid should fit snugly.

Sand the flange lightly to give the desired clearance.

It is desirable to taper the flange slightly, so that as the lid enters the opening, the clearance is greater, and as the lid seats it will fit the opening.

Fig. 380. Using a roundnose chisel shape the inside of the lid. Keep in mind that the inside of the lid is normally similar in shape to the outside.

During the removal of the wood, the center screw may appear. Turn right up to the screw. With care, the screw will not pull loose in the lid.

The inside shape of the lid must be flat or concave in order to use this method of turning lids.

Fig. 381. Sand the inside of the lid completely.

Remove the lid from the screw center.

Cut out a paper disc larger than the faceplate and place the paper disc over the screw center. This disc will prevent the faceplate from scratching the inside of the lid.

Screw the lid onto the faceplate.

Fig. 382. Turn the lid to the desired shape.

Do not turn the lid too thin.

Fig. 383. Select a small block of wood suitable for the knob.

Drill a pilot hole, and screw the block onto a small screw center.

Turn the block to rough dimensions, leaving a ¼" diameter plug on one end of the block.

Fig. 384. Cut the waste stock off the knob.

Bore a hole in the center of the lid, and glue the knob in place.

Fig. 385. Complete the turning of the knob.

Sand the outside of the lid.

Finish the lid, inside and out, with the desired finish.

Fig. 386. Bore a 3/8" hole, and insert a mushroom plug to cover the hole made by the screw center.

Fig. 387. Flat-bottom lids are fastened to the faceplate using the glue method.

Turn the lid to desired shape, then complete the finishing.

Separate the lid from the faceplate, remove the paper, and finish the bottom.

Fig. 388. Attractive lids for bottles can be made using the existing metal cap. The wooden cover over the cap will turn an ordinary bottle into an attractive kitchen storage container.

Select a piece of stock suitable for a cover.

Cut to rough dimensions and glue the stock to a scrap block screwed to the faceplate.

Fig. 389. Turn the stock to finished diameter.

Measure the diameter of the lid, and transfer the measurement to the stock.

Fig. 390. Bore a hole in the stock. The depth of the hole is less than the depth of the lid.

The diameter of the hole must be a tight fit for the metal lid.

Continue enlarging the hole until the lid can be force-fit into the hole.

Increase the depth of the hole until it is slightly deeper than the depth of the lid.

Fig. 391. Pressure fit the lid into the hole.

A small flat block may be used to tap the lid into place. Use care, and do not bend the lid.

The rolled edge of the lid should be snug against the wood.

Sand the edge of the wooden area.

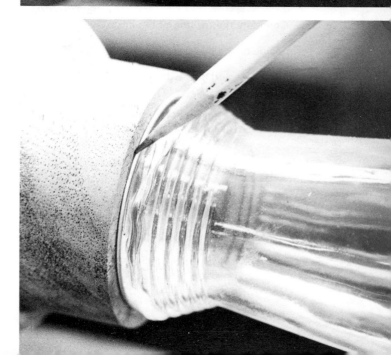

Fig. 392. Remove the lid and wooden cover from the faceplate, using a parting tool.

Bore a hole into the scrap wood on the faceplate. The hole should be at least ½ to ¾" deep, and a snug fit for the wooden cover.

Bore a hole in the center of the block about 1" in diameter, and through the block, exposing the opening in the faceplate.

Pressure fit the wooden cover into the large hole. The secret to a tight fit is a very slight taper on the side of the hole.

Fig. 393. Complete the turning of the wooden cover. The shape and size of the cover should be compatible with the shape and size of the jar.

Sand the unit.

Fig. 394. Remove the faceplate with the lid and cover from the lathe.

Insert a short piece of dowel through the faceplate and against the inside of the lid.

Tap gently to remove the lid and cover from the faceplate.

Fig. 395. The completed unit is now ready for finishing. Surface finishes or penetrating oil finishes are recommended.

Result: an attractive storage container from a relatively plain jar.

Small Round Boxes

Fig. 396. Small round boxes have a variety of uses. They may be used for spices, salt, sugar, and other dry ingredients in the kitchen. Children find the boxes popular for storing jewelry, coins or games such as jacks and marbles.

Larger round boxes may be used for cookies or candy jars. Whatever the size, this is a popular project.

One way to make a small round box is to use one piece of wood. The following sequence illustrates this method.

Fig. 397. Select a piece of wood suitable for the box, and turn to a cylinder.

Mount the cylinder to a faceplate, using the glue chuck method.

Turn the cylinder to the desired dimensions, then lay out the body and the lid.

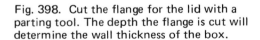

Fig. 398. Cut the flange for the lid with a parting tool. The depth the flange is cut will determine the wall thickness of the box.

Partially separate the lid from the body of the box.

Fig. 399. Turn the lid to desired shape, and sand it completely.

Separate the lid from the cylinder. Use a parting tool and complete the cut with a fine toothed saw.

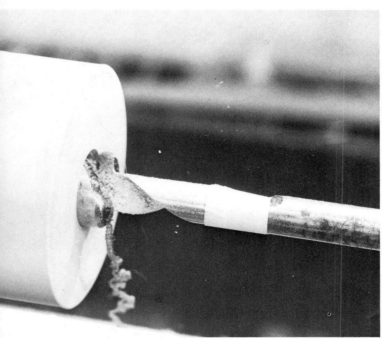

Fig. 400. Bore a hole the desired depth of the container. Note the tape on the bit to indicate the correct depth.

Fig. 401. Increase the size of the hole with a skew chisel or modified squarenose chisel.

Check the size of the opening frequently.

Stop cutting when the opening is slightly smaller than the flange on the lid.

If desired, a roundnose chisel may be used to shape the bottom of the box, and blend the bottom into the sides.

Fig. 402. Sand the interior of the box, taking care not to make the opening too large.

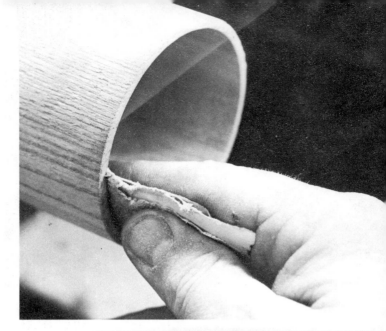

Fig. 403. Check the opening size with the lid.

At this time, the desired fit is one which requires the lid to be tapped into the opening with your hand.

Fig. 404. With the lid in place, complete the turning of the outside of the box.

Sand completely.

Fig. 405. Remove the lid, and sand the opening until the lid fits properly.

Fig. 406. The box may be left on the faceplate until finish is complete.

A strip of masking tape around the flange of the lid will allow the lid to be replaced, and stay in position until finishing is complete.

Use a parting tool and partially cut the box from the faceplate. Complete the removal of the box with a fine-toothed saw.

by Dale L. Nish

144

Turning Pepper Mills

Fig. 407. Pepper mills and salt shakers offer an interesting challenge to the wood turner. Designs and shapes can be varied to meet various decorator styles, while the small project such as this lends itself to the use of highly figured or exotic woods.

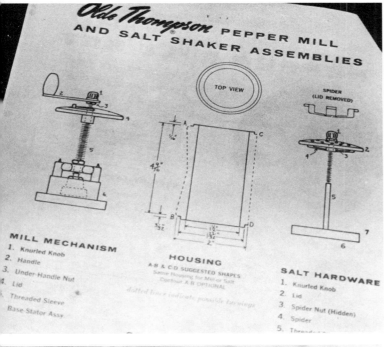

Fig. 408. If commercial hardware is to be used for the sets, carefully examine the specification sheet for measurements necessary to fit the hardware to the wood. Tolerances are close in this type of turning, and required measurements must be followed closely.

Fig. 409. Select a piece of stock at least ½" longer than net size, and of sufficient diameter to allow for the final shape of the turning.

Mount the stock and turn to rough diameter.

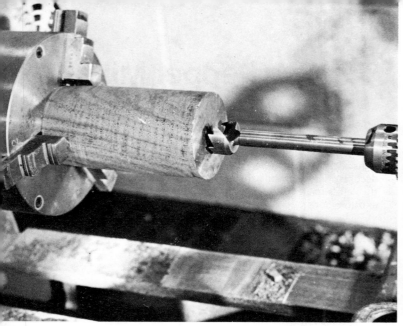

Fig. 410. Mount the cylinder in a three-jaw chuck and bore a hole the full length of the cylinder. Proceed carefully, as boring end grain is difficult. Best results are obtained when a small hole, for example 1'', is bored, then other larger bits used until the hole reaches final size—in this case, 1½''.

Do not attempt to drill the hole to the required size with the first bit used. The bit will vibrate and wobble enough that the hole will be over-size.

If a three-jaw chuck is not available, the blank may be bored *before it is turned to rough diameter.* This may be done on a drill press, or with a portable drill.

Fig. 411. A mandrel is a useful accessory for turning hollow projects, such as pepper mills. The mandrel shown was shop-made for this purpose. It consists of a threaded shaft and two

tapered plugs. One end of the threaded shaft is tapered and fits into the headstock of the lathe. A shoulder is left where the taper begins on the shaft. A pin projects through the shaft at a point against the shoulder. This pin fits into one of the plugs. The other plug slides over the shaft and is held in place with a threaded nut. The threaded end of the shaft is counterbored, to fit the cone end of a ball bearing center.

Fig. 412. The complete unit fits between the lathe headstock and tailstock. For turning a number of pepper mills, a mandrel is very useful.

One or two sets can be easily turned by turning a pair of tapered wooden plugs to fit into the bored hole in the pepper mill blank. The secret to success with tapered wooden plugs is a very slight taper with a snug fit. The plug should require a light tap with the hand to seat the shoulder of the plug against the stock.

Fig. 413. Mount the mill blank on the mandrel, with the right shoulder true and flat.

Set the calipers to the required length and mark the blank.

Use a parting tool and cut the blank to length.

Fig. 414. Set the calipers slightly over size and turn both shoulders to required diameter.

Cut to finished diameter with a skew or square-nose chisel.

In this critical operation accuracy is essential.

Fig. 415. Turn the outside of the mill to the desired shape. A template is useful for checking as pepper mills normally are used with a salt shaker of similar shape.

Fig. 416. Sand completely.

An oil finish may be applied while the work is still on the lathe, or the mill may be removed and finished using standard finishing methods. However, the mill should be mounted on the mandrel for sanding and polishing.

Fig. 417. The completed body is assembled with the hardware. This is a satisfying, useful, and beautiful project.

by Dale L. Nish

Segmented Ring Construction

Segmented ring construction is a method whereby bowls or similar containers may be constructed from pieces of stock not normally used for turnings; in fact, usually scrapwood.

This method offers practically unlimited opportunity for the turner to experiment with shape and color. Another advantage is the absence of end grain on the exterior surface of the turning, thus producing a surface uniform in color, texture and appearance.

Fig. 418. These bowls were constructed using the segmented ring method.

Fig. 419. Determine the number of rings required for the project, and rip the stock to uniform width. Wide pieces allow more flexibility in the final shape of the turning. A common width is 1½ to 2 inches.

The stock does not have to be uniform in thickness, although enough of one thickness is required to make eight sections.

Fig. 420. Set the miter gauge at 45°. Determine the length of segments required for the turning. The maximum diameter of the turning will be a little less than 2½ times the length of the long side of the segment.

Fig. 421. Sort the segments, and group them according to thickness, color, or other criteria which you may require.

Number the segments so they can be easily identified.

Fig. 422. Lay out each ring without glue, positioning segments as required for the design.

Fig. 423. Spread the end of one segment with a generous amount of glue. Spread the glue uniformly over the surface of the piece.

Fig. 424. Lay the two pieces on a flat surface, and slide the glued piece back and forth against the other segment. When glue uniformly appears along the glue line, move the pieces into final position, and carefully set aside to dry.

Fig. 425. Continue gluing the segments into pairs. Then let dry for several hours.

Fig. 426. Using the procedure described in Fig. 424, glue the pairs of segments into fours.

Fig. 427. Glue the fours into eights, which then make a completed ring. Let the rings dry overnight.

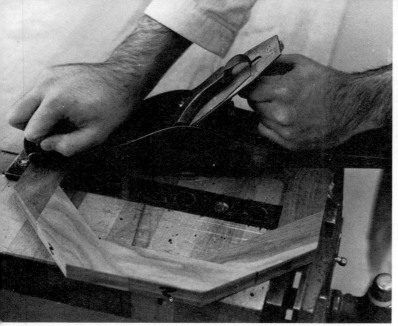

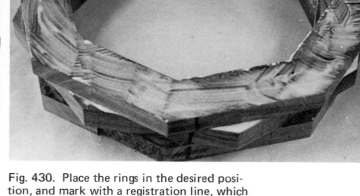

Fig. 428. Plane the surface of each ring flat and true. Do not use a surfacer or jointer, as the machine will tear the surface and edges of the rings.

Fig. 429. Mark the grain direction on each ring. This makes for easier assembly, and later on, easier turning as the grain will all be running the same direction.

Fig. 430. Place the rings in the desired position, and mark with a registration line, which helps keep the rings in alignment during gluing up.

Fig. 431. Place a generous amount of glue on one ring at a time. Spread the glue evenly, and build up the bowl.

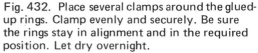

Fig. 432. Place several clamps around the glued-up rings. Clamp evenly and securely. Be sure the rings stay in alignment and in the required position. Let dry overnight.

Fig. 433. Cut out a plywood disc about the same diameter as the rings. Glue the disc to the segment which is to be the top of the bowl. Let the glue dry.

Center a faceplate on the disc and fasten in place.

Fig. 434. Mount the faceplate on the lathe, positioning the tool rest and rough turning the bowl to its maximum diameter. Do not attempt to shape the bowl at this time.

Fig. 435. Cut a rabbet at least ½" deep on the end of the bowl. The width of the rabbet depends on the final shape of the bowl. Make it at least ¼" wide, preferably more.

Check the rabbet to be sure it is true and flat.

Fig. 436. Cut out and mount a piece of stock suitable for the bottom of the bowl. Turn the stock to exact size. Check frequently for proper fit. The bottom must fit securely in the rabbet or the bowl will be off center on the base. Also, glue will not fill voids. A poor fit may cause the bottom to separate from the bowl, with a probable accident the result.

Fig. 437. Remove the bottom, complete with faceplate, from the headstock. Replace the bowl sides on the headstock.

Place a generous amount of glue in the rabbet, and insert the bottom piece into the rabbet.

Move the tailstock into position, using it to apply pressure and clamp the bottom into the bowl.

Leave on the lathe for at least 30 to 45 minutes, then remove the assembly and let dry overnight.

Fig. 438. Remove the faceplate from the bowl base. Use the parting tool, and cut about ½ to 2/3 the distance through the ring at the glue line between the top ring and the plywood disc.

Stop the lathe and complete the disc removal with a hand saw.

You are now ready to complete the bowl, using standard turning procedures.

Laminated Bowls

Fig. 439. This method of construction has been adapted for the woodturner from bowls produced by industry. The advantage to this procedure is the production of a bowl at minimum cost for materials. The complete bowl may be constructed from one piece of stock, ¾" or more in thickness, with the length and width necessary for the desired size of bowl.

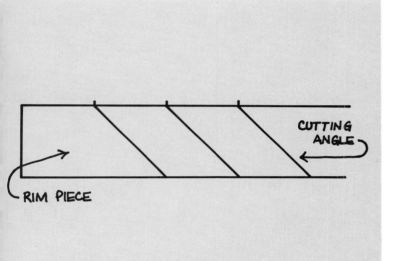

Fig. 440. The bowls may be produced in various shapes and sizes, the only limitations being equipment or stock available and the skill and ingenuity of the craftsman.

The basis of this method is that the angle of the side of the bowl is equal to the diagonal of a piece of the stock ¾" wide. The ¾" width is arbitrary, and could be more or less, but ¾" has been found satisfactory for most applications. Assuming ¾" is the width of a ring, with thickness variable according to the stock used, the diagonal establishes the angle for cutting the rings. By selecting stock of various thicknesses, the angle may be varied to suit the design requirements.

Fig. 441. Determine the stock dimensions necessary to complete the bowl. Thickness is most important.

Glue up the stock, edge to edge.

It is preferable to glue up an even number of pieces and leave the center joint open.

It is possible to glue up or use one solid piece, then rip into two pieces of equal width.

Surface the two pieces to uniform thickness and joint the center edge of each piece.

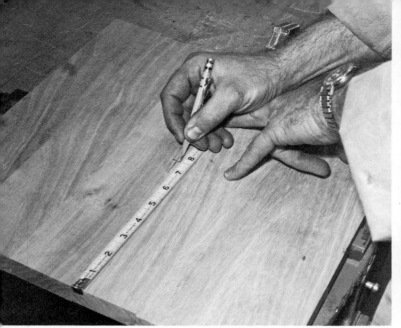

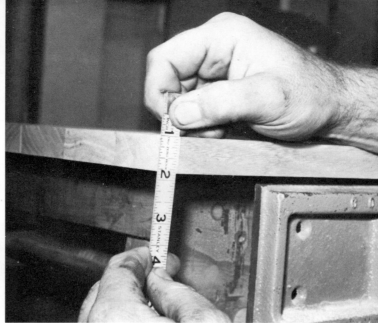

Fig. 442. Fasten the stock securely to the workbench and find the center point.

Fig. 443. Mark a circle the desired diameter of the bowl.

Fig. 444. Check the stock thickness.

Fig. 445. For a bowl with sides at 45°, lay out a series of points equal to the thickness of the stock.

Experience has shown that these points should be at least ¾" apart, regardless of stock thickness.

156

Fig. 446. Mark a series of circles on the stock.

The number will depend on the depth of the bowl and the size of the bottom.

Each segment will add *one* thickness of stock to the depth of the bowl.

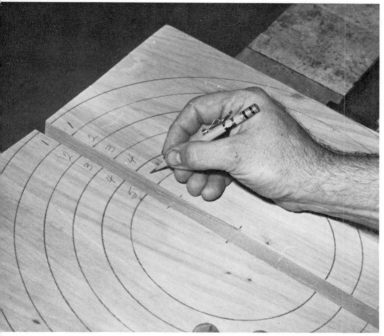

Fig. 447. Number the segments for ease of construction.

Cut out each half of the stock before tilting the band saw. This will allow sufficient stock for shaping the rim in various ways.

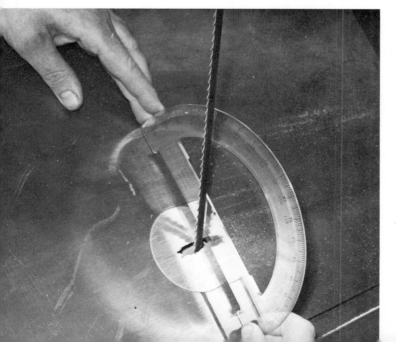

Fig. 448. Tilt the band saw to the required angle.

Check with a protractor.

Fig. 449. Lay the stock on the table and lower the blade guard until it clears the stock 1/8" to ¼".

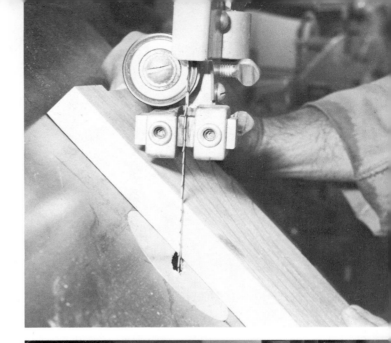

Fig. 450. Cut out each segment.

Work slowly and accurately.

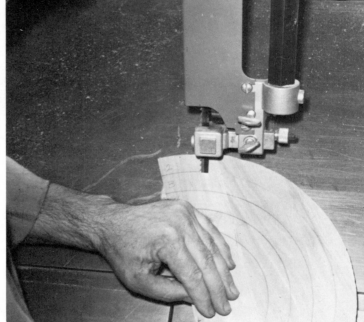

Fig. 451. As the segments are cut, carefully set aside until needed.

Fig. 452. The segments can be stacked to give a rough approximation of the final size and shape of the bowl.

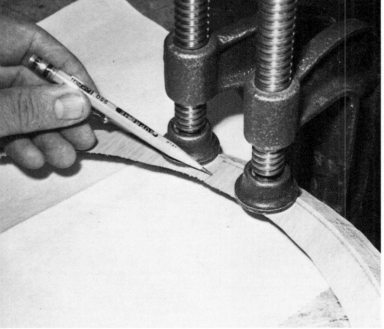

Fig. 453. The segments must be glued together to form rings.

Clamps may be used to hold them in position while the glue sets.

Fig. 454. If clamps are not used you may use a fast setting glue and hold each ring for a few minutes until the glue has set enough to hold the ring together.

Fig. 455. Let the glue set for 24 hours.

Lightly sand each glue line to remove excess glue.

The remainder of this sequence shows the use of a special clamp constructed for this type of project.

However, a lathe may be used as the clamping device if necessary.

Fig. 456. Cut out a circular piece of 3/4" plywood with a diameter greater than the diameter of the bowl.

Drive a nail through the center point.

Cut the head off the nail.

Fig. 457. Cut out a piece of paper the same diameter as the plywood.

Position the center of the paper over the point of the nail.

The paper is used to keep excess glue from sticking to the plywood.

Fig. 458. Draw a circle on the paper equal to the diameter of the bowl.

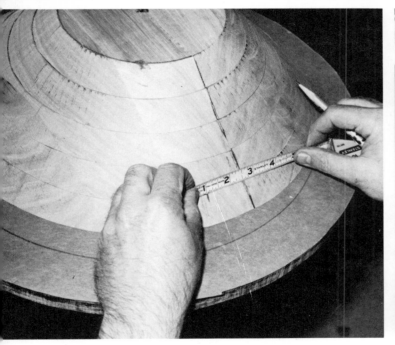

Fig. 459. Place the plywood circle on the clamp plate, with the nail shank entering the center hole.

This keeps the plywood circle centered on the plate.

Fig. 460. Place the circular segments on top of each other.

Measure from the center glue line the desired amount of offset.

The offsetting of the center glue line will strengthen the bowl and add to its appearance.

Fig. 461. Glue each segment to the one below.

Most woodworking glues are satisfactory; however, slow setting glues may work better for beginners. Epoxy is excellent.

If a white glue (polyvinyl) is used, you must work quickly.

Fig. 462. Distribute the glue evenly throughout the joint.

Fig. 463. Continue gluing until all the pieces are in place.

Fig. 464. Using a straightedge, check the sides for alignment.

Check all the way around and slide some of the rings, if necessary.

Fig. 465. Tighten the clamps.

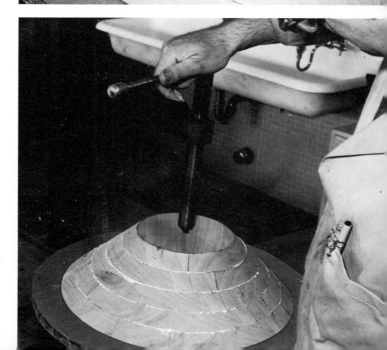

Fig. 466. Adjust the pointer on the gauge to a position just touching the bottom ring.

Rotate the bowl past the pointer.

If necessary, adjust the ring until it is centered.

Fig. 467. Check each ring for proper centering.

This is critical since any misalignment is doubled when the bowl is turned.

An improperly centered bowl may leave a thin finished wall, or may even cut through one side before the bowl is completely turned.

Fig. 468. Clamp the bowl in final position, and leave for at least 24 hours before turning.

by Dale L. Nish

Stave Construction

Stave construction is not unique to wood turning and has been used extensively in the construction of containers such as barrels and buckets.

The patternmaker also utilized this method to produce patterns for the casting industry. Stave construction has an application in wood turning, as the method allows the craftsman to produce beautiful turnings from small pieces of wood, with the absence of end grain and with a similar pattern or figure on all sides of the piece.

The procedure illustrated in the following sequence is but one way of producing a staved turning. Variations from the proceure will depend on the ability of the craftsman as well as the tools available.

Fig. 469. The compote bowl, as well as the other containers, was constructed from 12 pieces of wood, using stave construction.

Fig. 470. Lay out a full pattern of the turning and determine the diameter of the turning and the number of sides required.

Determine the width of each side piece from the table.

The thickness of the stock to be used is determined by the shape of the turning and the wall thickness desired.

Diameter of Turning	Number of Sides				
	8	10	12	14	16
2	27/32	21/32	17/32	15/32	13/32
2½	1 1/16	13/16	11/16	19/32	1/2
3	1 1/4	1		13/16	11/16	19/32
3½	1 15/32	1 5/32	15/16	13/16	23/32
4	1 21/32	1 5/16	1 3/32	15/16	13/16
4½	1 7/8	1 15/32	1 7/32	1 1/32	29/32
5	2 3/32	1 5/8	1 11/32	1 5/32	1
6	2 1/2	1 15/16	1 5/8	1 3/8	1 7/32
7	2 29/32	2 9/32	1 7/8	1 19/32	1 13/32
8	3 5/16	2 5/8	2 5/32	1 27/32	1 19/32
9	3 3/4	2 15/16	2 7/16	2 1/16	1 13/16
10	4 5/32	3 1/4	2 11/16	2 9/32	2
12	5	3 29/32	3 7/32	2 3/4	2 13/32
14	5 13/16	4 9/16	3 3/4	3 7/32	2 25/32
16	6 5/8	5 7/32	4 9/32	3 21/32	3 3/16

Fig. 471. Cut out the required number of pieces to rough length and width.

Tilt the circular saw blade to the required angle and cut the pieces to finished size.

Number of Sides	Tilt Setting
6	30°
8	22.5°
10	18°
12	15°
14	12.85°
16	11.25°
18	10°
20	9°
24	7.5°
30	6°

Fig. 472. Check the sawn edges for smoothness. If necessary, correct any irregularities with a belt sander or hand plane.

Caution: Do not change the angle.

Fig. 473. Lay out the pieces into the desired pattern, matching for color and grain pattern, or emphasizing any aspect of the wood you desire.

Number the pieces consecutively.

Fig. 474. Select a high-quality polyvinyl acetate glue, such as Franklin Titebond, and place a thin, uniform coating on each edge of the first two pieces to be glued together.

Slide the pieces together, then slightly back and forth until a uniform squeeze-out occurs along the glued joint.

Hand-hold for approximately one minute, then carefully set aside.

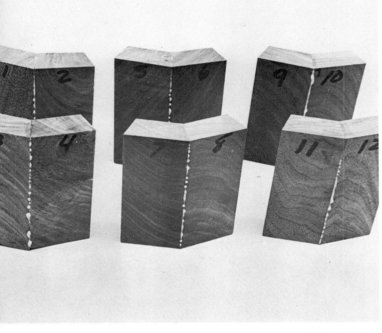

Fig. 475. Repeat the above procedure until all the pieces have been glued into pairs.

Set aside and let dry for at least one hour, preferably longer.

Fig. 476. Glue the twos into fours, using the procedure outlined in Fig. 474.

Glue two of the four-piece sections into one eight-piece section.

Set aside to dry for a few minutes.

Fig. 477. Hand fit the remaining section.

It is critical that this section fit perfectly.

Fig. 478. Glue and hold the remaining section in place.

Set the assembly aside to dry for eight hours, preferably longer.

Fig. 479. Determine the part of cylinder which is to be the top.

Using a disc sander or hand plane, flatten the top true and flat.

168

Fig. 480. Cut out a ¾" plywood disc the same diameter as the cylinder.

Glue and clamp the disc to the top of the cylinder.

Set aside to dry for at least eight hours.

Fig. 481. Center a faceplate on the plywood disc, and fasten securely.

Mounting the assembly on the lathe, rough turn the cylinder to a circular shape.

Fig. 482. True up the end of the cylinder.

Turn a rabbet on the inside edge of the cylinder.

The size of the rabbet will be determined by the desired final shape of the turning. However, the rabbet should allow the bottom to contact the maximum area of wood possible.

Fig. 483. Cut out a bottom piece for the turning.

The diameter of the piece should be at least ½" larger than the rabbeted opening on the end of the cylinder.

Fasten the bottom piece to the faceplate with screws, or use the glue method for fastening the bottom piece to the faceplate.

Fig. 484. Mount the bottom piece on the lathe and turn to the desired size.

Check frequently, as a tight fit is required.

Fig. 485. Remove the faceplate from the cylinder.

Place a generous amount of glue on all surfaces of the rabbet in the cylinder.

Slide the cylinder onto the bottom piece.

Fig. 486. Move the tailstock into position and use as a clamp.

Let the assembly set until the glue is thoroughly cured.

Cut the plywood disc from the top of the cylinder. Use a parting tool to partially cut through the cylinder.

Stop the lathe and finish removing the disc by cutting with a handsaw.

Fig. 487. Complete the turning in the usual manner.

by E. N. Pearson

Turning Goblets

Fig. 488. Goblets may be turned in a variety of shapes and sizes.

Fig. 489. The design is a matter of preference.

Fig. 490. For best results, use hardwood in making them.

Fig. 491. The wood should be selected for soundness, grain, and color.

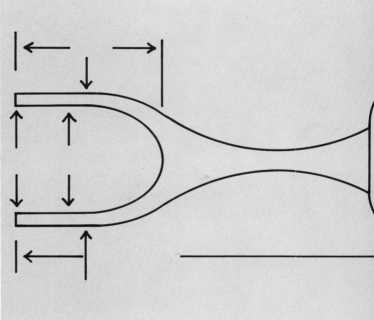

Fig. 492. For beginners, it is good practice to make a full size sectional drawing of the goblet.

The drawing should contain all the basic dimensions necessary for the completion of the goblet.

Fig. 493. Select a square solid block of wood, at least 1½" longer than the finished goblet, and thick enough to contain the goblet.

Fig. 494. Find the center of the block by drawing diagonal lines from corner to corner.

Select one end for the top of the goblet and make a center hole, using a nail set or a drill.

Drive the live center into the center of the other end.

Fig. 495. Mounting the stock in the lathe, rough turn the block until it is cylindrical in shape.

Do not remove more wood than is necessary.

Fig. 496. Turn a stub spindle on the end nearest the live center.

The stub is approximately 1¼" in diameter and about ¾" long.

Fig. 497. Select a scrap piece of stock, and lay out a circle approximately 5″ in diameter (the diameter will vary according to the size of the faceplate and stock to be turned).

Mark the center line and cut the piece to a circular size.

Fig. 498. Fasten the base piece to the faceplate, and turn a beveled edge.

Fig. 499. Bore a hole in the base piece.

The hole must be exactly the size of the stub spindle turned on the stock.

The hole may be bored with a skew chisel or by using a bit in the tail stock of the lathe.

Fig. 500. Check to see that the stub spindle fits snugly into the base piece.

Fig. 501. Place glue inside the hole in the base piece.

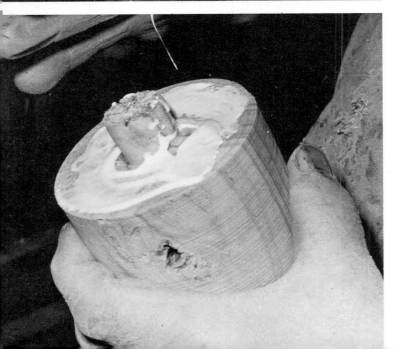

Fig. 502. Place glue on the stub spindle and on the shoulder of the workpiece.

Fig. 503. Place pieces together, then screw the faceplate onto the headstock spindle.

Slide the tailstock and dead center up to the workpiece.

Tighten the tailstock base clamp.

Turn the dead center into the workpiece.

Pressure from the dead center will act as a clamp, and keep the stock centered while the glue dries.

Leave the piece in place until the glue dries, preferably 24 hours or longer.

Fig. 504. Position the tool rest so the skew chisel will cut at the center of the stock.

Fig. 505. Start at the center, and work out toward the outside edge.

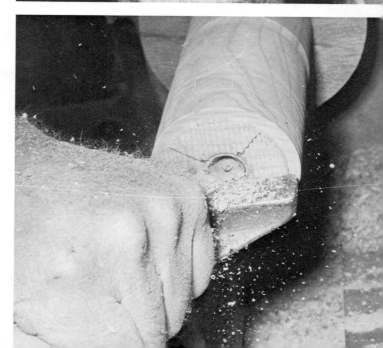

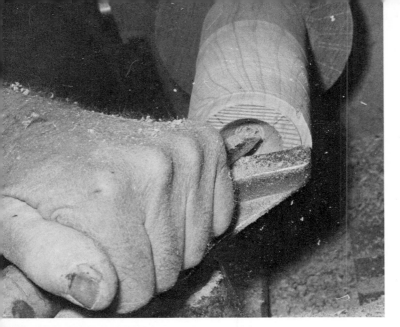

Fig. 506. Keep the chisel sharp, and remove the stock in small amounts.

Fig. 507. Continue using the skew until the opening has been roughed out to the proper diameter.

Start at the center again and proceed as shown above.

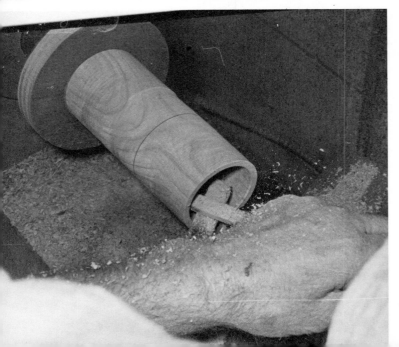

Fig. 508. Lay out a line indicating the correct depth of the goblet opening.

Continue removing material from the inside.

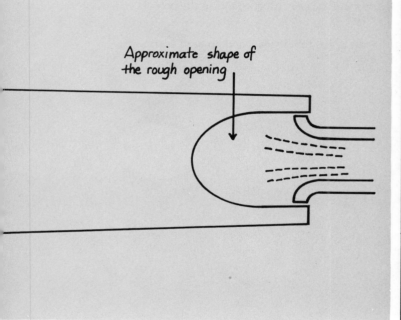

Approximate shape of
the rough opening

Fig. 509. When you have reached the desired depth, stop.

Fig. 510. Set the inside calipers to the diameter of the opening.

The calipers may then be used inside the opening to indicate the inside diameter dimension.

Fig. 511. Careful use of the calipers is essential, as the shape of the inside of the opening determines the outside shape of the goblet top.

Fig. 512. Turn the tool rest until the end is inside the goblet.

This will give good support for making the final finish cuts.

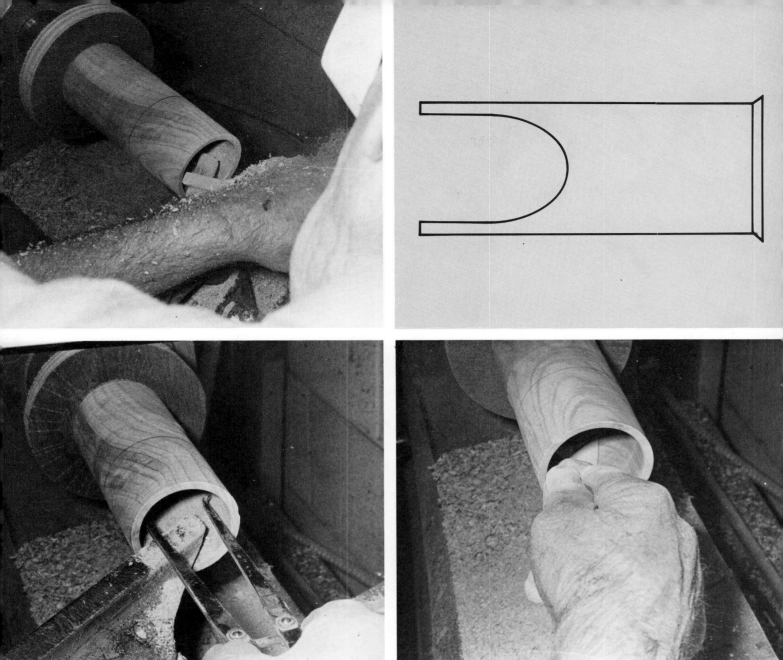

Fig. 513. Use a roundnose chisel to finish the inside of the goblet top.

Fig. 514. Carefully check the opening dimensions and the shape of the inside of the opening.

Fig. 515. The finished interior should be well-formed and smooth.

Fig. 516. Carefully sand the inside of the goblet.

Use various grits, but finish off with # 220 or # 280 grit.

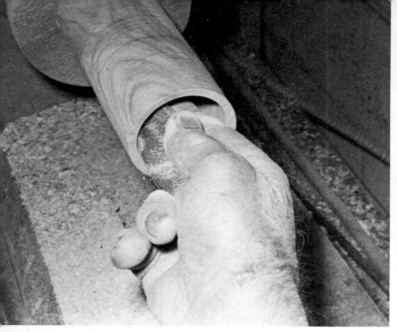

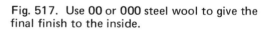

Fig. 517. Use 00 or 000 steel wool to give the final finish to the inside.

Fig. 518. Lay out the thickness of the bottom of the goblet.

Fig. 519. Use a parting tool and cut in on the *stem side of the bottom.*

An incorrect cut will ruin the goblet.

Fig. 520. Using a small gouge, or roundnose chisel, begin to shape the outside of the goblet top.

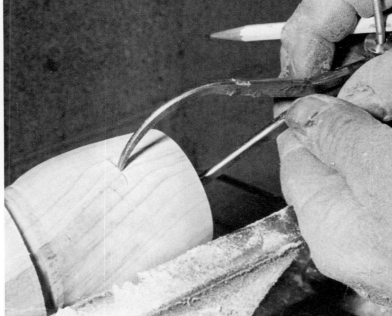

Fig. 521. Rough shape the top.

Fig. 522. Work slowly and carefully. Remove stock down to the edge of the opening.

Fig. 523. Set the calipers to the desired thickness for the walls of the goblet top.

Fig. 524. Move the calipers in until they are stopped by the thickness of the walls.

Mark a line at this point.

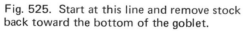

Fig. 525. Start at this line and remove stock back toward the bottom of the goblet.

Fig. 526. Check with the calipers, mark, and remove more stock.

Fig. 527. Remove enough stock from the stem area to allow you to continue working to the bottom of the goblet.

Fig. 528. Continue working toward the bottom, always checking carefully.

Fig. 529. Make the final smoothing cut with the skew chisel, using a shearing cut.

This cut may also be made by scraping, but it will require more sanding.

Fig. 530. The shaped top of the goblet, ready for sanding.

Fig. 531. Sand the outside of the goblet, using the same abrasive grits used for the inside.

Fig. 532. Carefully sand all the areas, as you will not be able to sand later.

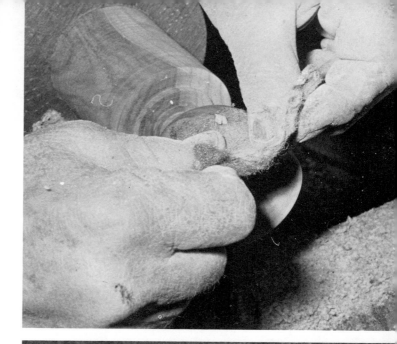

Fig. 533. Finish with steel wool (00 or 000).

Fig. 534. Rough out the base and stem for the goblet.

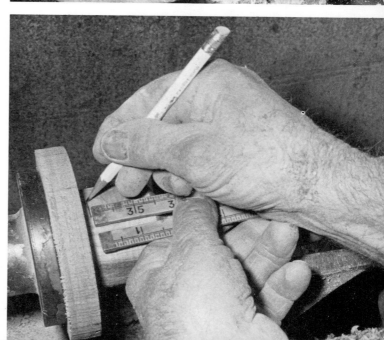

Fig. 535. Lay out and mark the total length of the goblet.

Fig. 536. Transfer the line around the base.

Fig. 537. Cut on the waste side of the line to the desired diameter for the base of the goblet.

Fig. 538. Remove excess stock until you reach the desired diameter for the base.

Leave enough of the cut that the line is not lost.

When the desired diameter is reached, use the parting tool and deepen the line dividing the base from the waste stock.

Using a roundnose chisel, continue roughing out the stem and base.

Fig. 539. Use the skew chisel, and cut a smooth shoulder on the bottom edge of the goblet base.

Fig. 540. Take the heavy cut at the base, then cut carefully, lightly tapering the cut as it reaches the thin part of the stem.

Fig. 541. Make the finish cuts on the stem and base of the goblet.

Fig. 542. A skew may be used to make a final finish cut on the goblet stem.

Caution: Skill is required to use the skew in making a shearing cut. If in doubt, omit this step.

Fig. 543. Sand the stem and base, using the same grit sizes as before.

Do not exert pressure, as the goblet is fragile.

188

Fig. 544. Finish with steel wool.

Fig. 545. The completed goblet, ready for application of the finish.

Fig. 546. The goblet is left fastened to the faceplate until the finishing is complete.

Sanding between finish coats is done on the lathe.

Final polishing is done on the lathe.

Fig. 547. After finishing is complete, the goblet is bandsawed from the faceplate.

The bottom is sanded smooth and a felt disc is glued to the bottom of the goblet.

by Dale L. Nish

Project:
Candle Lamps

Fig. 548. Candle lamps can be made in various shapes and sizes.

Some have standard globes, which can be purchased from hardware stores.

Fig. 549. Some have light fixture globes, which can be purchased from lighting fixture stores.

Fig. 550. Design the candle lamp.

One way is to cut the design out of folded paper. Try various shapes, until you find one that satisfies you.

Lay out the basic dimensions, keeping in mind that the size of the top is determined by the base diameter of the globe.

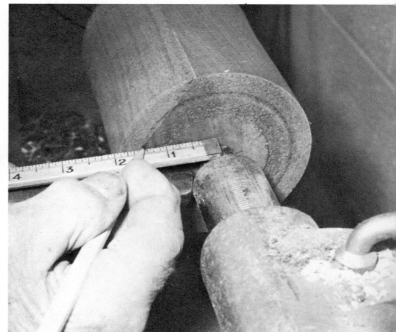

Fig. 551. Select a piece of stock large enough for the candle lamp.

It may be necessary to glue up stock to obtain the desired thickness.

Lay out the diagonals and center punch the ends.

Fig. 552. Place the stock in the lathe with the top toward the tailstock.

Turn the stock to its rough dimension.

Fig. 553. Use a parting tool and square the end of the stock.

Fig. 554. Determine the diameter of the base of the globe.

Lay out the diameter of the globe on the end of the stock.

Rotate the stock against the pencil, marking the groove around the end of the cylinder.

Fig. 555. Position the tool rest against the end of the cylinder.

Cut a shallow groove on the end of the cylinder.

Use a parting tool 1/8" thick.

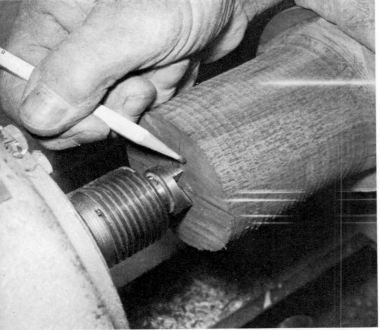

Fig. 556. Mark the live center position on the left end of the stock.

This will allow you to reposition the stock into its original position.

Fig. 557. Remove the stock, and check the fit of the groove to the globe.

Replace the stock and, if necessary, adjust the fit of the groove.

Continue removing the stock and checking with the globe until you are satisfied with the fit.

Fig. 558. Place a mark on a thin piece of wood (1/8" or less).

The mark should be ¾" from one end.

Use this mark to check the depth of the groove.

Deepen the groove until it is ¾" deep.

Fig. 559. The lamp globe should fit snugly into the end of the stock.

Fig. 560. Using the parting tool, remove most of the center of the stock.

Leave a wall 1/8 to 3/16" thick between the groove and the center of the top.

Do not remove the stock to the point that the wood supporting the dead center is weakened. Leave a piece ¾" to 7/8" in diameter.

The depth of the center is ¾".

Fig. 561. Lay out the basic measurements for the top of the candle lamp.

Fig. 562. Use the parting tool and cut to the desired depth, checking with the calipers.

Fig. 563. Lay the skew chisel on its back, and cut a V-groove at the point where the cove begins.

Fig. 564. Lay the gouge on its side and establish the correct cutting angles. (See "Turning Stock Between Centers: Using a Gouge to Make Coves or Grooves," page 46.)

A roundnose chisel may also be used to cut this cove, and may be more suitable for the beginner.

If a gouge is used, insert the tip of the gouge into the V-groove, and begin the cut.

Fig. 565. Cut the cove to its final shape, leaving only enough stock for a fine finish cut.

Fig. 566. Using the gouge, reduce the top to the required diameter.

The wall thickness between the groove and the outside of the top will vary according to the design you have chosen.

Fig. 567. Lay out the width of the beads and cut a V-groove for each bead.

Fig. 568. Use a skew chisel and, with a shearing cut, turn the two beads. (See "Turning Between Centers: Making Beads with Skew Chisel, Cutting Method," page 50.)

Fig. 569. Finish the cove, using a sharp round-nose chisel.

Take a fine finish cut, which will remove any small defects in the surface of the cove and leave a smooth finish.

Fig. 570. Lay out and rough shape the bowl of the candle lamp.

Use a gouge and make a shearing cut.

Fig. 571. Turn the shoulder of the bowl with the skew.

The skew is handled the same way as when turning a bead.

Fig. 572. Turn a stub spindle on the end next to the live center.

The stub is approximately 1¼″ in diameter and ¾″ long.

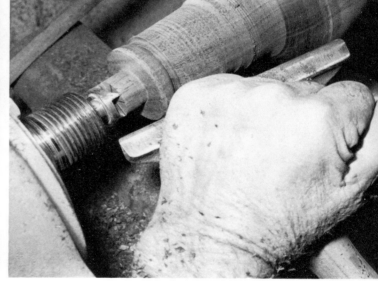

Fig. 573. Cut to the depth of the large diameter required for the lower end of the candle lamp.

Use the parting tool and calipers.

Fig. 574. Rough out the remaining length of the stock.

Then, using a gouge, make a series of short, shearing cuts.

Fig. 575. Smooth out the cylinder and proceed with the remaining cuts.

Fig. 576. A bead is usually made where the spindle fits into the base.

Fig. 577. The other cuts are a matter of choice.

Using the appropriate tools, continue turning the candle lamp.

Fig. 578. Cut the coves with a sharp gouge, then finish with the roundnose chisel.

Fig. 579. Check the shoulder by the stub spindle.

Use a straightedge to be sure the shoulder is flat, or even slightly concave.

Fig. 580. Sand the turning completely. Use a variety of grits, but finish off with # 220 or # 280 grit.

Be particularly careful not to sand away the sharp edges of shoulders or misshape the beads.

Fig. 581. Use 00 or 000 steel wool for the final smoothing.

Fig. 582. Remove any remaining scratches by sanding with the grain, using very fine (# 280) abrasive paper.

Fig. 583. Lay out the base and cut to rough shape, using the band saw.

Fasten the base to a faceplate and turn to the desired shape.

Lay out the hole which will receive the stub spindle.

Fig. 584. Bore the hole for the stub spindle.

True the face of the base so the shoulder of the turning will fit flat against the base.

Fig. 585. Sand the base to its final smoothing.

Finish with steel wool.

Fig. 586. Place glue in the hole in the base.

Place a small amount of glue on the shoulder next to the stub spindle.

Insert the stub into the hole and position the two parts with regard to grain direction.

Fig. 587. Move the tailstock into position, and use the lathe as a clamp.

by E. N. Pearson

Project Section

Fig. 1. Dried flower holder (Deanna Nish), 1¾" x 3½", walnut, off-center turning

Fig. 2. Candle holder (Dale L. Nish), 5" x 4½", walnut

Fig. 3. Candle holder (Dale L. Nish), 5" x 4", walnut

Fig. 4. Bud vases (Randy Nish), 3'' x 4'', walnut

Fig. 5. Box (Dale L. Nish), 3¼'' x 4'', walnut, turned as a one-piece turning

Fig. 6. Covered bowl (Dale L. Nish), 3'' x 7'', Pau Ferro

Fig. 7. Candle holder (Dale L. Nish), 2½'' x 8¼'', walnut

Fig. 8. Goblet (Dale L. Nish), 3¼″ x 2¼″,
cherry

Fig. 9.   Planter (Dale L. Nish), 9½'' x 11'', walnut

Fig. 10. Spice wheel (Dale L. Nish), 17'' diameter, Shedua

Fig. 11. Candle lamp (Dale L. Nish), 18'' x 13'', walnut

Fig. 12. Covered bowls (Dale L. Nish), 3¾"
x 9½", walnut, right; 4" x 7½", walnut, left

Fig. 13. Ice bucket (Dale L. Nish), 5" x
7¼", walnut, staved construction

Fig. 14. Compote (E. N. Pearson), 6½" x
8½", walnut

Fig. 15. Nut bowl (Dale L. Nish), 7¼" x 6",
walnut, turned as two separate pieces

Fig. 16. Container (Dale L. Nish), 6½" x 3",
metal lid set in vermilion wood

Fig. 17. Goblet (E. N. Pearson), 2¾" x 7",
walnut base used to repair broken stem

Fig. 18. Salt and pepper shakers (E. N.
Pearson), 2½" x 4½", ebony and maple

Fig. 19. Goblet (E. N. Pearson), 3" x 7½",
walnut

Fig. 20. Table lamps (E. N. Pearson), 18" x
8", laminated from several kinds of wood

Fig. 21. Bowl (Dale L. Nish), 2" x 6",
walnut; turned green, then seasoned

Fig. 22. Bowls (Randy Nish), front, 5" x 13"; rear, 7" x 18", walnut, segmented ring construction

Fig. 23. Chip and dip tray (Dale L. Nish), walnut, olive rings around the ceramic dish

Fig. 24. Fiddleback stool (Don Nish), 6" x 14", pine

Fig. 25. Bud vase (Dale L. Nish), 2¼" x 6", English walnut, oval turning

Fig. 26. Salt shaker and pepper mill (Dale L. Nish), 5" x 2 3/8", claro walnut, turned on a mandrel

Fig. 27. Salt and pepper shakers (Randy Nish), 2¼" x 3", walnut

Fig. 28. Salt and pepper shakers (E. N. Pearson), 5" x 1½", walnut, turned in two pieces, then assembled

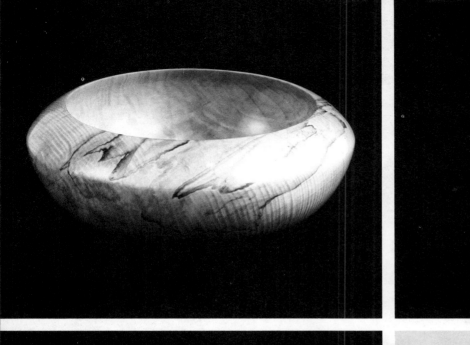

Fig. 29. Bowl (Dale L. Nish), 5½" x 12",
silverleaf maple

Fig. 30. Bowls (Brian Nish), front, 1¼" x
6"; rear, 2" x 6", silverleaf maple

Fig. 31. Bowl (Brian Nish), 3½" x 3",
poplar

Fig. 32. Bud vase (Dale L. Nish), 7¾" x
3¼", poplar, oval turning

Fig. 33. Toothpick holder (E. N. Pearson),
2½″ x 3¾″, laminated

Fig. 34. Bud vase (Dale L. Nish), 6¼″ x
3¼″, cherry, off-center turning; turned from
three centers on base, with top staying at the
same center

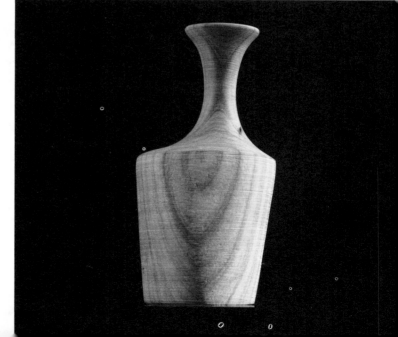

Fig. 35. Tier tray (Dale L. Nish), 9½'' x 11'', shedua

Fig. 36. Tier tray (Dale L. Nish), 6'' x 10'', walnut, turned in three pieces

Fig. 37. Bowl (Dale L. Nish), 3'' x 7½'', walnut, off-center turning by changing stock position on faceplate

Fig. 38. Dish (Dale L. Nish), 4½'' x 11'', walnut, two bowls with side sections removed; bowls glued to a center section; the side pieces become the handle

Fig. 39. Bowls (Dale L. Nish), front, 3″ x 6″,
walnut, solid stock; rear, 5″ x 5½″, laminated
walnut pieces; top of each bowl handshaped
after turning

Fig. 40. Goblets (E. N. Pearson), myrtlewood

Fig. 41. Bowls (Dale L. Nish), large bowl
4½'' x 10'', silverleaf maple

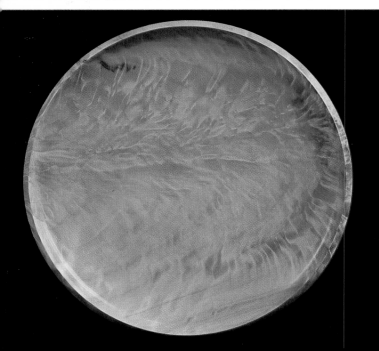

Fig. 42. Tray (Dale L. Nish), 1½'' x 11'',
poplar crotch figure

Fig. 43. Bowl (Robert Stocksdale), 4" x 8½", ash (opposite page)

Fig. 44. Bowl (Robert Stocksdale), 4" x 7½", English walnut

Fig. 45. Salad bowl (Robert Stocksdale), 11" x 23", Honduras mahogany

Fig. 46. Bowl (Robert Stocksdale), 3" x 7½", desert ironwood

Fig. 47. Bowl (Dale L. Nish), 5″ x 11″,
silverleaf maple

Fig. 48. Laminated bowl (Edwin C. Hinckley),
6″ x 11″, walnut

Fig. 49. Laminated bowl (Dale L. Nish),
4″ x 8½″, walnut

Fig. 50. Bowl with hand-carved exterior (Robert G. Trout), 6" x 12", teak

Fig. 51. Bowl (Robert G. Trout), 7" x 5",
walnut

Fig. 52. Laminated bowl (Robert G. Trout),
6" x 6", olive wood

Fig. 53. Bowl (Robert G. Trout), 3" x 4",
cocobolo

Fig. 54. Covered bowl (E. N. Pearson),
5" x 9", walnut

Fig. 55. Mortar and pestle (Randy Nish), 2½'' x 4'', walnut

Fig. 56. Bowls (Dale L. Nish), front, 3¼'' x 9'', off-center turning; rear, 3½'' x 9½''

Fig. 57. Bowl (Dale L. Nish), 4'' x 4½'', walnut

Fig. 58. Covered container (Dale L. Nish), 3¾'' x 4½'', maccassar ebony, staved construction

Fig. 59. Covered dish (Dale L. Nish), 4½" x 5½", walnut, staved construction

Fig. 60 Pin holders (Dale L. Nish), mother porcupine, 4½" x 7"; family, 2½" x 4½"; cork bodies with walnut faces

Fig. 61. Covered pot (Dale L. Nish), 4" x 4½", walnut

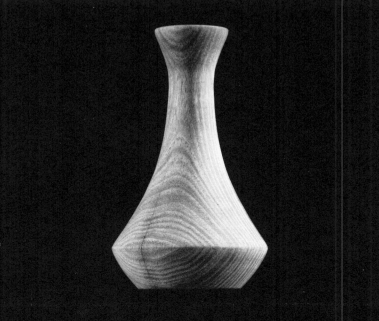

Fig. 62. Jack box (Dale L. Nish), 3¼'' x 3'', ash, one piece container

Fig. 63. Bud vase (Dale L. Nish), 5'' x 2¾'', black locust

Fig. 64. Bud vase (Dale L. Nish), 5″ x 3″, box elder, antique red finish

Fig. 65. Salt and pepper shakers (E. N. Pearson), 1¾″ x 5″, walnut, turned in two pieces, joined at brass ring

Fig. 66. Goblets (E. N. Pearson), 3¼″ x 7½″, walnut

Fig. 67. Platter (Dale L. Nish), 1½'' x 10¾'',
zebra wood, edge-shaped after turning

Fig. 68. Bowl (Dale L. Nish), 3'' x 9½'',
Siberian elm

Fig. 69. Plate (Dale L. Nish), 1¼'' x 10'',
walnut

Fig. 70. Plate wall plaques (Dale L. Nish),
1¾'' x 10'', decorative plates set in walnut
frames

Fig. 71. Salt and pepper shakers (E. N. Pearson), 1½" x 4¾", walnut, turned in two pieces

Fig. 72. Sugar bowl (Dale L. Nish), 6" x 7¼", box elder, finished in antique blue—a reproduction of an Early American sugar bowl

Fig. 73. Top (Dale L. Nish), 2" x 5", maple

Fig. 74. Jewelry box (Dale L. Nish), 3½" x 7", angico

Fig. 75. Dish (Dale L. Nish), 2¼" x 18", claro walnut

Fig. 76. Serving tray (Dale L. Nish), 9½" x 16", teak

Fig. 77. Serving tray (Dale L. Nish), 10¾" x 14", walnut; crotch figure, tray-shaped after turning

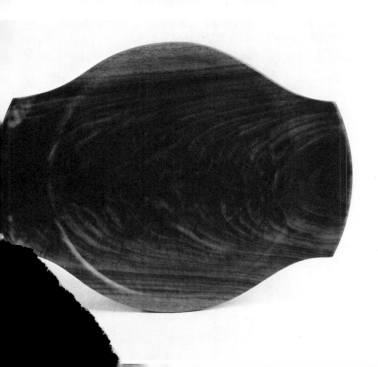

Fig. 78. Compotes (Dale L. Nish), walnut,
large, 9½" x 8"; small, 7¼" x 6"; staved
construction

Fig. 79. Candle lamp (Dale L. Nish), 11" x 6", claro walnut base

Fig. 80. Perfume holders (Dale L. Nish), 2½" x 3¾" and 4" x 2¼", walnut and pau ferro

Fig. 81. Vase (Dale L. Nish), 11½" x 5½", walnut, turned from limbwood, with the inside of the vase the same shape as the outside; wall thickness approximately ¼ inch

Fig. 82. Goblets (Dale L. Nish), cherry,
middle-sized goblet is 3¼″ x 2½″

Fig. 83. Table (Paul N. Pearson), walnut and cherry, segmented top, with solid stock legs

Fig. 84. Corner shelf (E. N. Pearson), 50'' x 22'', walnut. This unit may be completely disassembled—all joints being pressure fit

Fig. 85. Table lamp (Dale L. Nish), 20'' x 8½'', walnut, turned from limbwood

Fig. 86. Mirror frame (E. N. Pearson), 24'' x 24'', walnut, split turning

Fig. 87. Bowl (Dale L. Nish), 3½" x 9½",
Siberian elm, turned green and stabilized
with P.E.G. 1000

Fig. 88. Bowl (Joe B. Pearson), 2½" x 5½",
sycamore

Fig. 89. Bowl (Craig Hinckley), 2½" x 4",
birch

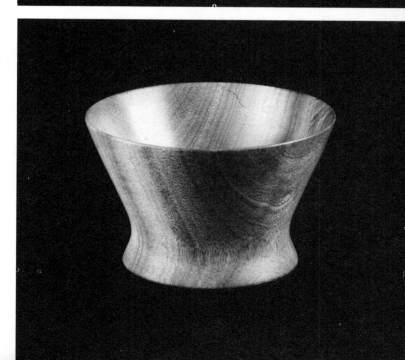

Fig. 90. Bowl (Dale L. Nish), 5" x 11½", walnut

Fig. 91. Jewel box (Scott Hinckley), 2¾" x 5½", African mahogany

Fig. 92. Carving board (Dale L. Nish), 1¼" x 12", walnut, off-center turning on faceplate

Fig. 93. Candle lamps (Dale L. Nish), 8½" x 4", walnut, reproductions of E. N. Pearson originals

Fig. 94. Weed pots (Dale L. Nish), walnut, large, 6'' x 5½''; small, 4'' x 7''; openings were cut out after pot was turned

Fig. 95. Candle holders (Scott Hinckley), 6'' x 5'', walnut

Fig. 96. Bowl (Scott Hinckley), 2¼'' x 6'', olive

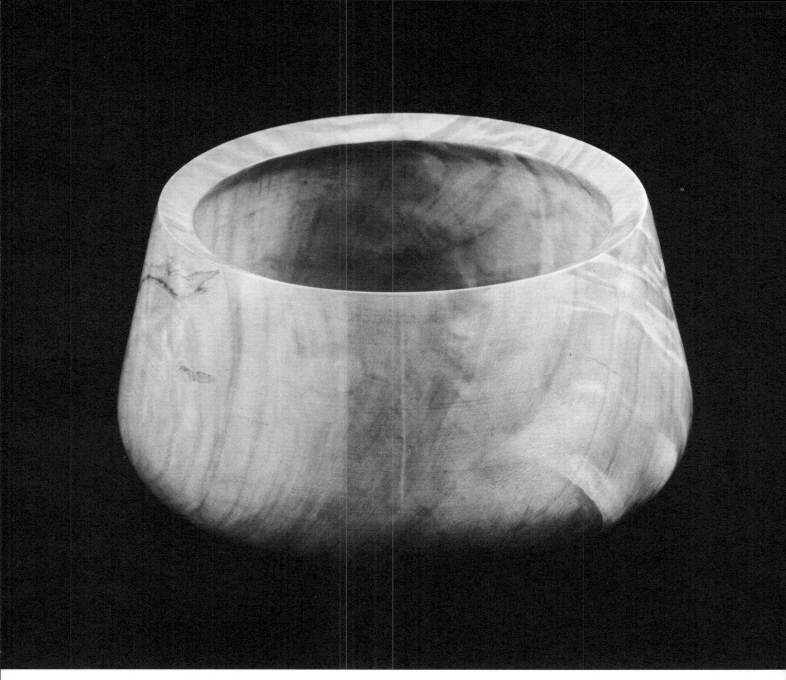

Fig. 97. Bowl (Dale L. Nish), 4½″ x 8½″,
poplar

Fig. 98. Bowl (Dale L. Nish), 4½'' x 13¼'',
goncalo alves; segmented ring construction

Fig. 99. Bowl (Dale L. Nish), 5¼'' x 11'',
shedua, segmented ring construction

Fig. 100. Pencil holders (Darrel Nish), 3'' x
4½'', walnut and ash

Fig. 101. Bowl (Edwin C. Hinckley), 4″ x 8½″, walnut

Fig. 102. Salt and pepper set (Dale L. Nish), 3 5/8″ x 2¼″, maple and ebony

Fig. 103. Bowl (Robert G. Trout), 4½″ x 10″, teak (*Photo courtesy of artist*)

Fig. 104. Bowls (Robert G. Trout), small
bowl, 2¼'' x 4'', tulip wood (*Photo courtesy
of artist*)

Fig. 105. Bowl (Robert G. Trout), 5'' x 10'', teak (*Photo courtesy of artist*)

Fig. 106. Bowl (Robert G. Trout), 3'' x 6'', walnut (*Photo courtesy of artist*)

Fig. 107. Covered container (Robert G. Trout), 5'' x 8'', walnut (*Photo courtesy of artist*)

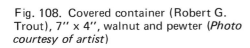

Fig. 108. Covered container (Robert G. Trout), 7" x 4", walnut and pewter (*Photo courtesy of artist*)

Fig. 109. Candle lamps (Dale L. Nish), 10" x 7½", cherry

Fig. 110. Miniature turnings (R. Ladell Harston), walnut; largest of these is 5½" high

Fig. 111. Goblet (R. Ladell Harston), 2" x 5½", walnut

Author and Consultant

Dale L. Nish, author of *Creative Woodturning,* is a totally involved woodworker/teacher whose vocational-professional interests overlap completely his avocational interests. Continually in search for new methods and procedures, he spent the summer of 1975 in Europe visiting design centers, wood manufacturing operations, and craft shops. He is in constant demand as a workshop leader and has been a visiting professor at Washington State University. His students are continually impressed at his ease and speed in turning a rough chunk of wood into a work of art. I have enjoyed working with him during the past few years.

Edwin C. Hinckley

E. N. Pearson, technical consultant for *Creative Woodturning,* is one of the master woodturners of the nation, whose turnings are collector's items. Of even greater importance, however, has been his willingness to help and encourage anyone interested enough to seek his advice. His life has been devoted to teaching and his touch has extended to thousands during his many years of instructing in the public schools and in universities. Mr. Pearson is retired, but works daily at his lathe in a cabinet shop owned by his son, Byrd N. Pearson, also a master woodworker and stockmaker.

Dale L. Nish

Index